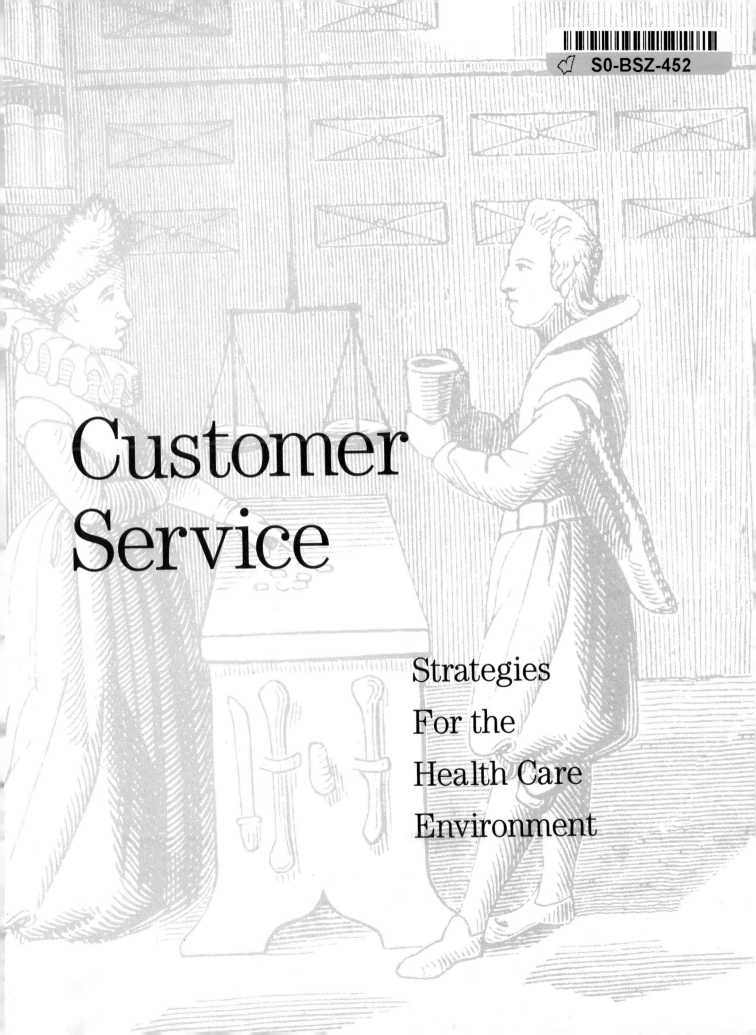

Customer Service

Strategies For the Health Care Environment

The Health Insurance Association of America
Washington, D.C. 20004-1204

ISBN 1-879143-57-7

Contents

Figures   vii

Foreword   ix

Preface   xi

Acknowledgments   xiii

About the Author   xv

Part One: Creating a Customer-Driven Organization

1 The Business Philosophy of an Outstanding Health Care Organization   3

2 Customer Service That Makes a Difference   7

3 Customer Service: Your Most Important Product   15

4 Taking Down the Seven Barriers to Outstanding Customer Service   25

5 Strategies for Delivering Quality Service   33

Part Two: Communicating with Customers

6 Tools for Clear Communication   51

7 When Nothing You Do Seems to Work   57

8 Telephone Strategies   63

9 How to Learn About Your Customer   69

Part Three: Improving Customer Service

10 How to Verify the Quality of Your Services   77

11 How to Analyze the Service Cycles of Your Business   83

12 Criteria for Evaluating the Quality of Service   89

13 How to Monitor Four Key Problem Areas   93

Part Four: Managing, Staffing, and Training

14 How to Manage Your Customer Service Operation   99

15 Building a Customer Service Team That Works   107

16 Negotiating with Your Health Care Customer   113

17 Creating Efficiency in Your Health Care Business Environment   123

18 The Management Challenge: Hiring Right and for the Right Reasons   127

19 Developing a Customer Service Training Program   133

Part Five: Handling Customer Complaints

20 The Impact of a Complaint   141

21 The Most Common Complaints   145

22 The Value of a Complaint   149

23 Comments to Avoid Saying to Customers   155

24 Solutions to Customer Complaints   161

25 Problem Solving Strategies   165

Part Six: Understanding Accreditation

26 What Accreditation Is and What It Is Used For   171

27 The Three Major Accrediting Bodies in Insurance and Managed Care   183

28 Accreditation Standards That Relate to Customer Service   199

29 How Accreditation Affects Customer Service   213

Appendix A: 50 Tips for Quality Customer Service   221

Appendix B: Accreditations Available by Accrediting Agency   223

Appendix C: Overview by Accrediting Agency of the Major Standard Areas   225

Notes   229

Key Terms   231

Index   233

Frequently Asked Questions About the HIAA Examination   239

HIAA's Courses and Professional Designations   241

Other Books from HIAA   243

The HIAA Insurance Education Program   245

Figures

Chapter 7
Figure 7.1   Sample Letter of Apology

Chapter 10
Figure 10.1   Sample Customer Service Survey Script

Chapter 19
Figure 19.1   Sample Employee Training Record
Figure 19.2   Employee Survey Questionnaire

Chapter 22
Figure 22.1   Sample Copy of a Complaint Report

Foreword

This book is published by the Insurance Education Program of the Health Insurance Association of America (HIAA).

HIAA is the nation's most prominent trade association representing the private health care system. Its more than 300 members provide health, long-term care, dental, disability, and supplemental coverage to more than 123 million Americans. It is the nation's premier provider of self-study courses on health insurance, managed care, long-term care, and related topics.

The mission of HIAA's Insurance Education Program includes the following goals:

- to provide tools for insurance company personnel to use in enhancing the quality and efficiency of services to the public;

- to provide a career development vehicle for insurer employees and other health care industry professionals; and

- to promote general understanding of the role and contribution of the health insurance industry in the financing, administration, and delivery of health care services.

The Insurance Education Program provides the following services:

- a comprehensive course of study in the fundamentals of health insurance, medical expense insurance, supplemental health insurance, long-term care insurance, disability income insurance, managed care, health insurance fraud, HIPAA, and customer service in the health care environment;

- certification of educational achievement by proctored examination for all courses;

- programs to recognize accomplishment in the industry and academic communities through course evaluation and certification, which enable participants to obtain academic or continuing education credits; and

- development of educational, instructional, training, and informational materials related to the health insurance and health care industries.

The Health Insurance Association of America (HIAA)
Insurance Education Program
1201 F Street NW, Suite 500
Washington, DC 20004-1204
800-509-4422
Web: www.hiaa.org
Email: mgrant@hiaa.org

Preface

Many providers in the health care industry pay extraordinary attention to clinical treatment programs, research and development, reimbursement issues, lobbying, staffing, and marketing communications. These are all important areas, but to stay truly competitive in the current health care environment, we need to place more emphasis on customer service. The patients and clients who are the end-users of our products and services are the reason we make policies and implement procedures. They influence administrative and clinical practices. They are our incentive for creating new programs and services. And to meet the demands of today's savvy health care consumers, we must continually evaluate and improve the programs we deliver and the systems we use to bring our services to the public.

The customer is the final judge for what works and what does not. Without customers we have no business. They are not an interruption in our work, but the reason for our existence. Not only an important issue for frontline staff, dedication to excellent service must receive the full commitment of all employees. From nurse manager to corporate director, office supervisor to customer service representative, everyone must support quality service—it is the lifeblood of the organization.

Many consumers will spend more money on health care than on any other purchase they make in a lifetime, including home, car, vacation, or financial investment. As providers of health care products, it is in our best interest to develop an ongoing relationship with our customers by educating, informing, and consulting with them, and thereby becoming an important and trusted advisor.

Customer Service Strategies for the Health Care Environment explores key ingredients for keeping customers satisfied. Whether we work in the insurance industry or home care, medical equipment manufacturing or case management, a hospital or rehabilitation center, this book will motivate us to improve service. The intent is to generate thought, discussion, and action. Readers will find practical strategies, tools, and exercises designed to increase their awareness of customer service issues affecting every department within an organization. They will also learn about the accreditation process, what major accrediting bodies look for in customer service, and discover the value accreditation brings to the overall delivery of quality health care.

To help readers evaluate their own performance and the activities of their company, discussion questions and exercises are interspersed throughout the text. Many of the exercises can become the focal point for training sessions or staff meetings. Completing the exercises will help readers analyze customer-related issues, identify problems in business or clinical practices, and recognize strengths. The material has a wide range of applications. Some of the questions can be developed into individual surveys and directed to every employee in the company, providing the impetus for discussions at corporate meetings, future training programs, or even for a comprehensive customer service audit of each department.

How can we become a customer-driven industry? This is the question health care providers must address as they read and engage in the practical applications of this book. *Customer Service Strategies for the Health Care Environment* encourages readers to take a closer look at all aspects of their business and to set and achieve the highest standards for quality service.

Louis Feuer, MA, MSW
President, Dynamic Seminars & Consulting, Inc.

Acknowledgments

Author

Louis C. Feuer, MA, MSW
Dynamic Seminars & Consulting, Inc.

Contributors and Reviewers

John A. Boni
Physicians Mutual Insurance Company

Mary Ellen Conway, RN, BSN
Capitol Health Care Group

Gregory F. Dean, JD, CLU, ChFC
Health Insurance Association of America

James E. Del Fosse
Bankers Life and Casualty Company

Nancy Eckrich
Trustmark Insurance Company

Mary Jo Ginty, MBA
MJG and Associates

Gregory Johnson
Health Insurance Association of America

Alexandra Kermisch
Mutual of Omaha

Susanne Lanza
Health Insurance Association of America

Terry R. Lowe, HIA, CLU, ChFC, FMLI, FLHC, ACS
State Farm Insurance Companies

Melissa A. Shelton
AultCare

Cyndi Snyder, MBA
Project Management Professional

Carol A. Woltz
Principal Life Insurance Company

Robert R. Worobow
Trustmark Insurance Company

Carol A. Woltz
Principal Life Insurance Company

Robert R. Worobow
Trustmark Insurance Company

Editors

Michael G. Bell
Joyce C. Meals

About the Author

Louis C. Feuer is recognized in the health care industry as a leading expert on customer service. The President of Dynamic Seminars & Consulting, Inc., Mr. Feuer provides sales, marketing, and customer service training to many of the nation's leading health care corporations. A prolific contributor to the professional literature, his articles have appeared in many journals, including *The Case Manager, Caring Magazine, The Journal of Hospital Marketing, Home Care, Home Health Products, Independent Living,* and *Medical Product Sales.* He also received special national recognition at the American Booksellers Convention for his book *White-Collar Stress,* published in 1987. A frequent keynote speaker at industry meetings, Mr. Feuer presented lectures at the Medical Case Management Conference, Case Management Society of America, and Medtrade, the world's largest medical trade show and conference, to name just a few. Mr. Feuer has a Master's Degree in Social Work.

Contributors

Mary Jo Ginty is an independent consultant and owner of MJG and Associates. She is also co-founder and CEO of Managed Care Consultants Association; co-founder and COO of the Virtual Training Company; advisory board member of National Managed Healthcare Congress; and a member of the editorial board of several trade organizations. Ms. Ginty holds a Bachelor's Degree from Ursuline College and an MBA from UCLA.

Cyndi Snyder is a project manager for the health care industry and a professional trainer. She has worked in the managed care industry for over 10 years, managing mergers, acquisitions, product releases, and accreditation surveys. Ms. Synder also designs, develops, and leads classes in project management for a wide range of clients. A certified Project Management Professional, Ms. Synder holds a Master's Degree in Business Administration.

Maureen Cirbee Yadgood is President of Maureen Yadgood & Associates, a consulting firm specializing in regulatory compliance; clinical program planning and start-up; operational reviews; and development of clinical and management systems. Ms Yadgood is a nationally known speaker on accreditation as well as outcomes management and has published several journal articles on these topics. She earned a Bachelor's Degree in Nursing and a Master's in Nursing Administration from Marymount University.

Creating a Customer-Driven Organization

1

The Business Philosophy of an Outstanding Health Care Organization

Objectives

- Identify who is responsible for quality service.

- Understand why a sound business philosophy focuses on the customer.

- Recognize key elements essential to all interactions with customers.

Every successful company must be sensitive to customer service at all levels of the organization. You won't hear the comment "It's not my job" at first-rate companies. Quality customer service is not the exclusive responsibility of the customer service department or an issue for managers to address—it's everyone's issue! No one should be excused from customer service training. If you notice that customer service training programs are being scheduled for other staff members and you have not been invited to attend any of the programs, the time to speak up is now.

It doesn't matter if you work in utilization review, claims adjustment, billing, marketing, or operations; everyone has to know how to deal effectively with customers. Do not ever be fooled that in your position you are shielded from the real revenue producers. Also remember that customers do not exist only outside the walls of your organization. Many are sitting right next to you. They include colleagues that you interact with everyday: people who sit with you on committees, work with you on developing new programs, and share the responsibilities for servicing clients. Your colleagues are your customers, too. How you treat them will ultimately affect the way they treat you. Often we treat people we work with the same way we treat customers. Think about your interactions with your colleagues as you consider what the customer may be experiencing.

Quality service must become habit-forming. Practicing with your coworkers will help you set the stage for providing the same caliber of service to those who have decided to spend their hard-earned dollars with you. Regardless of the day of the week, the time of day, or the person you are talking with, you must use the very same customer service strategies with everyone—all the time.

While health care companies provide a wide variety of services, the manner and tone with which these products are offered to your market should be similar. Customers expect a high level of service and caring—no matter what product they are purchasing. And most likely they will have little interest in how you are feeling or care about the pressures you are experiencing. They are usually focused only on what they need or want.

We continue to learn our best practices from many different health care organizations. By observing operations, talking to managers, and attending corporate gatherings, we have found that outstanding service providers share some common traits. Here are three key elements we've identified that characterize the way outstanding companies do business:

- **Quality service** is the guiding principle that permeates organizational philosophy, training, and work done by all employees throughout the company;

- **Customer-oriented people** on the front line listen and respond to the needs of the customer; and

- **Customer-friendly systems** make it easier for the customer to do business with the provider.

Take a moment to review your company's mission statement and ask yourself these questions: Does the statement reflect management's concern and dedication to service? Does your organization have programs and meetings scheduled that are dedicated to the issue of quality service? Do you have a quality assurance or total quality management program for addressing customer service issues?

Corporate Commitment to Customer Service

As you analyze the service in your company, answer these important questions:

1. Do you know where your mission statement is posted? ___Yes ___No

2. Was a mission statement discussed in the first week on the job? ___Yes ___No

3. Do you believe management cares about the customer? ___Yes ___No

4. Does your company have a customer service training program? ___Yes ___No

5. Have you ever taken time to read your mission statement? ___Yes ___No

6. Does it include comments about the commitment to customers? ___Yes ___No

7. Can you identify programs developed to make it easier for the customer? ___Yes ___No

8. Do you believe management is committed to customer service? ___Yes ___No

9. Do you hear people talk about the great service offered, but you are not sure it is everyone's concern? ___Yes ___No

If your company has developed a customer service program, consider the impact of that program on the customer and the organization. It is always disappointing to spend hours at meetings planning a program that does not solve problems for customers, or, even worse, may actually create more problems. Has this ever happened where you work?

Your Customer Service Program

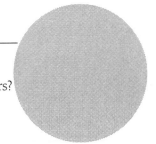

If a customer service program or procedures program has been developed in your department or company, how would you describe its acceptance by your customers? (*select one*)

_____ Very much appreciate

_____ Appreciate

_____ Do not know about the program

_____ Did not appreciate the change

_____ Expressed concern and dislike

Was everyone trained and educated about the program?

Was it a program that was in effect for a short time and now forgotten?

Are you ready to suggest a new customer service strategy?

Briefly describe how it would work.

To whom will you go to present your suggestions?

Will management listen to your recommendations?

If your organization's mission statement does not refer to the importance of customers and you have not developed programs that benefit the people you are in business to serve, your company may need to reevaluate its mission, to create a customer-driven operation. Moreover, you may need to initiate changes to the programs you now have in place if your services have not been well received by your targeted population. Can you think of any changes you would suggest?

Some programs may need immediate termination. To stay competitive in today's market-place, providers of health care services should harness the power of the customer. If your systems are not meeting customer needs, stop, rethink, and consider their extinction. Take some advice from Sam Walton, who saw the customer as the "true boss." The Wal-Mart founder said the customer makes a decision everyday about where he will spend his money. Walton urged employees to provide the service that would allow them to remain in business. In the health care industry, you may find your survival at stake—unless you deliver what the customer wants.

Review Questions

1. Who is responsible for customer service?

   _____
   _____
   _____
   _____

2. Why is it important to deliver quality service to colleagues?

   _____
   _____
   _____
   _____

3. What are the three characteristics shared by outstanding service providers?

   _____
   _____
   _____
   _____

4. How did Sam Walton describe the customer?

   _____
   _____
   _____
   _____

2

Customer Service That Makes a Difference

Objectives

- Identify two primary reasons customers maintain business relationships.

- Recognize the value of consistent service.

- Understand the complexity of the customer, who is often an unwilling participant in the health care system.

Issues related to customer service increase as an organization grows. It should be evident that the competition wants to expand its share of the market. And that the market has become more crowded with new managed care organizations, clinics, rehabilitation centers, and home care companies opening their doors everyday.

To succeed, you will need to work harder at distinguishing yourself from your competitors. The health care consumer has many choices. There are dramatic changes in all segments of the industry, including managed care, long-term care, insurance costs, and Medicare/Medicaid reimbursement. In spite of the challenges, providers are still developing programs and bringing new products and services to the marketplace. With people living longer and living well, the industry's customer base is growing and so is the number of providers targeting the needs of the older population.

When new health care organizations enter the field, owners and corporate executives are often enthusiastic about the service components of their business. There is competitive pressure to provide extraordinary service. Competition can and should inspire you to do some strange and wonderful things. You may find yourself working late to make sure a customer report is done or arranging an evening appointment with a family, at a time when it is convenient for them.

What competition does best is to force you to examine all aspects of your business. You must begin your service evaluation now, since most of your competitors have evaluated your business prior to opening their own doors. They have heard about how you handle patients; what you say on the telephone; the instructions you provide to patients; how you handle managed care negotiations; and especially how you respond to complaints.

How to Become a Preferred Business

A rule to remember: *People do business with people they like.* That's why outstanding customer service makes a difference. Just because a patient has a serious illness does not preclude his ability to make choices, change providers, or look for new insurance. The patient's commitment to a hospital, physician, or allied health professional may be influenced by how he feels about the service, and whether he thinks he was treated with respect and dignity during his personal interactions with attending staff.

Without customers you have no business. Customers are not an interruption in your workday. They are the reason you remain in business. Your products and services cannot sell themselves. Ideally, you have people who care about the customer at the helm. People in your company and those you come in contact with—they make the *business* happen.

Many business relationships continue to flourish in spite of price increases and industry changes. In a survey, more than 100 case managers were asked how they selected the companies with whom they did business. Not one of the respondents cited clinical expertise as the primary reason for their choice. The case managers who completed the questionnaires named characteristics like service, attitude, reliability, and professionalism as factors influencing their decisions. Some commented that company representatives "did what they promised," "stood by their products," and "cared about keeping their customers happy." Notice that all of these comments refer to a very positive personal experience the case manager had with the organization in question.

When our customers first hear our voices or meet with us in our offices, they make rapid judgments about whether they want to do business with us. People make quick decisions about what they like and dislike. They often fail to give a health care provider much time to prove himself. If the wait is long, the office staff unfriendly, or the conversation about scheduling an appointment too complicated, the customer may consider moving on to the next health care provider.

Your Last Call: A Reality Check

1. When you last called your physician's office, do you recall the sound and attitude of the person you initially spoke with? Can you describe it?

2. Did you get the feeling you were interrupting them?

3. Did the person you spoke with sound as if he/she had more important tasks to attend to?

4. Did you have a negative attitude the last time you picked up the telephone?

5. Have you ever caught yourself sounding somewhat rushed on the telephone, thinking the call coming in was arriving at just the wrong time?

6. Have you ever not apologized to the customer for sounding abrupt?

7. Have you ever found yourself dropping the phone in anger?

8. Are there customers that you would prefer never called again?

9. Who don't you like calling but cannot avoid speaking with?

10. Have you stopped doing business with someone because of attitude?

11. Who are they and why?

Did you find yourself answering yes to any of these questions? If you have experienced some of the situations referred to, you are probably also aware of the feelings your customers may have experienced when dealing with your company. In fact, you may also have experienced the same problems others are having in providing quality service. If problems exist, in time these issues will affect your customers and how they approach working with your department. You may need to intervene now before a complaint letter from an angry customer arrives on your desk.

Customer service is a complex issue. Never lose sight of the importance of how you present yourself to customers and the value you bring to the exchange. Good customer service does not come naturally. Most employees need constant reminders about the importance of quality service plus strategies for how we can make it happen. Too often we forget just how much poor service can negatively impact business relationships.

Customer Service as a Way of Life

When we talk about service, we are talking about a concept or a philosophy that may not come naturally to everyone. It has to do with the way people treat each other. For many of us, concepts about service did not become an issue we had to grapple with until we started our own business, took our first job, or began spending the money we worked so hard to accumulate.

Providing outstanding customer service should become a way of life. Its importance is evident as you handle all your professional responsibilities. Its presence will ensure the success of your organization. Too frequently we hear companies say they want their fair share of the business. Keep this in mind: Your competitor doesn't want his fair share—he wants it all. And he will get it all if you forget why you are in business.

How you personally respond to the customer during all interactions sets a tone for the future success of the relationship. You may need to change your attitude, place a smile on your face, and watch what you say. You cannot allow inappropriate comments to generate negative perceptions. You must avoid making any comments about customers to other customers. Do not make negative comments about your competition. (With the growth of mergers and acquisitions, someday you could be working for the company you are now complaining about.) Being friendly is the best approach.

Keep It Simple and Sincere

A second vitally important rule to keep in mind is: *People do business with people who are easy to do business with.* In recent years we are finding health care providers and business owners eager to share with customers their cell-phone numbers, e-mail addresses, home telephone numbers, and pager and beeper numbers. With all of this information the customer should be able to reach you at a moment's notice. You have no excuse for not responding in a timely manner.

So often you overhear people tell someone to call them any time. You may have said that yourself. Then you call them only to realize they have made a promise to you they are unable to keep. If you are difficult to reach, you will soon be extinct in the business world. Most calls coming to your desk are from other professionals seeking information that is needed within a short period of time. No customer will continue to do business with people who are unresponsive. While a lot of companies provide employees with all the latest in communication technology, it is apparent many people and companies are having problems using the technology to the best business advantage.

Technology and Customer Access

- What technology should your company install to help customers?

- Have you been trained on new equipment and what it can offer?

- Are you able to access your messages easily?

- Do you have a policy regarding timely response to messages?

- Does your telephone system help or hurt your business?

- Can the customer easily access a designated employee?

Since customer service does not come naturally, constant reminders are in order. Try placing signs on the office wall, near telephones, in meeting rooms, or even in restrooms—wherever the most people will see and read the message. We all need to be committed to doing whatever works to keep employees mindful of the importance of excellent service.

Posting Customer Service Reminders

As you consider placing customer service reminders in your office, answer these questions:

• Where would you place the reminders?

• Would management be supportive of a companywide customer service effort?

• What messages would you place on the signs?

Maintain Consistency

Quality service must be constant. Customers expect the same level of service at all times. To stay in business, you must meet customer expectations—even when you are short-staffed, on a Monday after a long holiday weekend, or if you have more business today than you can possibly handle. Office problems should not become a problem for your customer.

Customers come back when they know what to expect and you always meet their expectations. How do you think chain food restaurants keep millions of people showing up at the counter each day or at the drive-through window? It doesn't matter where the establishment is located. It could be Pittsburgh, Pennsylvania, or Paris, France. McDonald's hamburger is the same the world over. Customers know what to expect. Do your customers know what they can expect before they call on your company?

Some days your service will be better than others. At times you may find yourself rushing your customer through the order-taking process. This is not acceptable. Customers quickly become aware of how they are being treated, and retain this information for later recall, especially when they consider doing business with you again. Times have changed. Patients are no longer loyal to one physician. The family doctor who took care of you since childhood is a thing of the past. A patient in the hospital may have to check her arm bracelet to recall the name of her physician.

Outstanding customer service must be extended regardless of the time or the day. It must be expressed during every interaction, with the customer in your office, on the telephone, in her hospital room, or at his home. Even on the weekends, customer service cannot afford to take a vacation. It is a performance that takes no breaks or vacations, certainly not as long as you continue to have any interactions with your customers. Anyone who understudies your position must also carry on in the same tradition.

Customers often show up at the most inopportune times: when you first come into the office, as you are about to have lunch, or when you have already turned off the computer and the office lights. Sometimes they even have the nerve to come in to the office or call just as you are on your way out the door.

Do you recall a day when you were just going out the door and the telephone rang? Did you pick it up, rushed and annoyed that you had to answer the phone? Envision yourself standing next to the telephone with your briefcase in your hand, just wishing the caller would talk faster, tell you exactly what he wanted, and get finished. Didn't you feel like saying, "Just talk faster and tell me what you want." Unfortunately, customers do not always operate on your time schedule. You need to realize that it is often important to meet their needs in their time frame rather than require them to conform to your schedule.

Develop Positive Business Habits

If a company wants to make quality service consistent and routine, then it should develop a system that rewards and reinforces positive business habits. Publicly acknowledging an employee who has exceeded customer expectations sends a message to other staff about how management values excellent performance. Complimentary letters from customers sent to you or your colleagues should be copied, posted, and circulated throughout the office. It signifies to staff what customer service habits management and customers expect, and recognizes those who are working hard to place your company ahead of the competition.

For some, customer service training began in nursery school with recitation of the **golden rule**: "Do unto others as you would have them do unto you." Your employer looks for people who have learned common human courtesies and continue to use them everyday. Have you learned the common courtesies, like respect and concern for others? While these are habits many of us learned in childhood, some of us may have forgotten their value.

Put yourself in your customer's shoes. Most people who access our services are reluctant participants in the health care system. They had not counted on being sick, or having to call your company for assistance. No one plans to be ill or expects to become one of your customers. Until they experience a health problem, people don't think about needing a nurse, a rehabilitation center, or a bedside commode. They had not considered purchasing a new health insurance policy. They may be uninformed, have to call your office several times concerning the same issue, yet expect the same polite response from your staff.

Many of us work in companies that have developed programs and procedures without ever studying and analyzing the effect of our protocols on customers. The more you research, talk to, and learn from your customers, the better able you will be to build a profitable health care business.

Another consideration is that the customer may be ordering services/products on behalf of someone else. You need to be even more patient with these caregivers. They may not have all the information you need to process the request immediately. These caregivers or advisors may have some problems accessing information that is important to you in your efforts to meet the real customer's needs. If they are an end-user (patient) of your services/products, they may be confused, having experienced some physical problems that have necessitated their call. They may not even be sure what they need or how you can help. You may have taken calls from people in pain, physically and mentally. Your patience and understanding in all of these situations will be a winning customer service strategy. Each customer brings to the business relationship a unique set of personal and professional concerns. You need to take the time to learn about these concerns and how you may need to deal with them as you work to assist someone who needs your help.

You must be aware that patients and referral sources have their own set of stressors to deal with and their own set of short- and long-term goals. The professional may need assistance in managing a very difficult patient population. The patient may need help reaching goals on his or her path to achieving personal independence. In each case, these people have called on your firm hoping you will help them in a unique way, and they expect you to respond with patience and concern.

You will continue to be faced with an interesting array of customers, each with a unique set of concerns, but all expecting the same common courtesies. Delivering outstanding customer service makes the difference.

Exceeding Expectations

- Explain what you or your colleagues have done for customers above and beyond what was described in your policy and procedure book. What was offered because it was good for the customer?

- Is there anything I (we) do or information I provide for my professional customers to make their work easier?

- What service do we provide that separates us from our competition?

Review Questions

1. What are two primary reasons customers maintain business relationships?

_____

_____

_____

_____

2. Name characteristics case managers cited for selection of service providers.

_____

_____

_____

_____

3. How can a company develop positive business habits?

_____

_____

_____

_____

4. Name one of the reasons McDonald's is so successful.

_____

_____

_____

_____

5. What can managers do to reinforce quality service?

_____

_____

_____

_____

3

Customer Service: Your Most Important Product

Objectives

- Understand how service is evaluated.

- Outline what affects the way service is provided.

- Analyze why limiting the number of customer contacts may enhance customer satisfaction.

Today, employees working in the health care industry must be knowledgeable about a wide range of services and products. You must learn about new programs and keep up-to-date on regulations that affect your business. Many products are complex and require detailed descriptions. You will be fielding questions from customers with different backgrounds and levels of experience and education. To help your customers make informed decisions, you will need a thorough understanding of product features and benefits.

You may be asked to explain options to a client who is interested in purchasing a long-term care insurance policy, or talk authoritatively about rules and regulations that you did not write. With many companies subcontracting for a variety of client services, you may be further challenged to learn about programs that are on your menu of services.

While it is important to have product knowledge, a more essential task is to learn about the service needed to bring these products to the market. It may not be listed in your company brochure, but service is your most important product. Yet it is probably the area that receives the fewest training dollars and very little funding for research and development. Most people think quality service is something that just happens. Now is the time to get a better understanding of service as a product and to learn about its intangible properties. Here are some guidelines to shape your thinking, feeling, and sensitivity.

Service is produced at the time the product/program is delivered to the customer.

Talk is cheap. At some companies, customer service is treated like the weather. It is talked about as if it were something out of everyone's control. Service is not something that can be stored, saved, or packaged for delivery at a later date. People seem to talk about it a lot, but do nothing to make sure it happens. You can write protocols, policies, and manuals, but service becomes a reality only when you have the opportunity to offer it to your customers.

Do not just talk about great service—provide it. It cannot be tested, analyzed, or studied until it actually happens. Customer service cannot be saved for a later time or delayed for delivery at a later date. Since it is your most important product, it must be showing at all times. There is little value in talking about how well you provide quality service unless you can prove it. Your competition may be the winner in gaining the attention of your customer. You can be assured that once the customer receives your great service she will be quick to spread the message of your good deeds.

Wonderful service will have a powerful impact on the marketplace. It will be the reason customers continue to do business with you. They will come to appreciate the service you offer, as much as the clinical expertise or state-of-the-art products that you provide. You must create an atmosphere where customers feel appreciated and are eager to share stories of their positive experiences with future customers.

Consider Your Feelings

Discuss and describe how you responded in these situations:

- What was it like when you arrived late for an appointment? How were you treated and what were you told?

- Have you ever complained about the service in an office and no one seemed to care?

- Have you ever returned a product to a store where they made you feel that you were the problem?

- Have you ever complained about a meal in a restaurant and the waiter was shocked that you were unhappy?

The quality of the service depends upon the customer's personal experience at the time of the interaction.

Customer service is often interpreted based upon the experiences of a human interaction. It has to do with perception of an image, one's feelings and the interactions between one person and another—how two people feel and think about each other at the very time the business interaction is taking place.

For example, the customer's interaction with the insurance company representative at any particular time may be either positive or negative depending on many factors. These factors may include how confident you sounded on the phone in your desire to help the customer. Did you make eye contact when speaking with the customer in your office? Did you welcome him with a smile and thank him for calling you? Did you allow yourself to be disturbed by supposedly more important issues as you were trying to determine exactly what the customer wanted? Did any of these elements interfere with your interactions?

Have you ever found yourself or a colleague talking on the telephone when you actually wanted to be doing something? Did you see the caller as an annoyance in an already busy day? This same person, handling a call on yet another day or possibly another hour may provide a totally different approach to the customer. Timing can make all the difference in this customer's service experience. There is no limit to the number of issues that can deter the development of a positive customer service experience.

Your Best and Worst Work Times

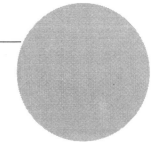

- What time of day are you the busiest?

- Do staff members feel more pressured on specific days of the week?

- What days of the week are these?

- What have you done to make sure the service your company provides does not suffer because of internal office problems?

Your business interactions can be enhanced with a smile, a kind gesture, and a show of respect for your customer. Those first few seconds when you meet the customer for the first time, either in person or on the telephone, are so important to the ultimate direction of the relationship. Here are some important behaviors: (1) smile, (2) make favorable comments regarding how much you look forward to your working together, (3) offer your hand in greeting, (4) talk about the customer's needs not just the provider's, and (5) express concern about meeting the customer's needs and creating a positive working relationship.

Customer Conversations

- What is the greeting you use when you pick up the telephone?

- How do you close a telephone conversation? (What are the last words you used?)

- What is the greeting you use when someone enters your office?

While later chapters will offer suggestions for telephone greetings, remember when picking up the telephone to immediately remind people about the name of the company they have called and also your own name. Make sure to close all telephone conversations by telling the caller that you appreciate hearing from them. Where we need the most help is on what happens between the greeting and the closing!

Brief but important expressions can have long lasting effects on your important relationships. Comments such as "we appreciate your business," "we are anxious to make you happy," and "we understand your concerns" are all valuable expressions. Good customer service requires you to be sensitive to everything that happens during, as well as surrounding, this interaction. Almost anything can positively or negatively affect the way the relationship evolves. The first interaction with the customer will set the stage for whatever is to come. You need to be aware of what your customer is projecting, judging from her attitude, appearance, and mood. If you have any sense that the relationship is not going well, you are probably right and something should be done. Go with your senses since they are usually correct.

Stop fooling yourself and move in another direction if the relationship does not appear to be going well. Try to repair the damage before the entire industry knows about the turmoil. When attempting to maintain a good relationship, you will need to use all of your senses. Similar to early warning signals you may have in other personal relationships, you will almost instantly realize if there is tension between you and the customer. You know when she is upset, concerned, and irritated. The patient may be frustrated in her attempt to contact you or to understand how her new insurance policy affects the coverage of a long-term illness. While there is much to learn about a relationship, you need to be sensitive to what the customer may be feeling.

Watch how the customers respond to you. Are you upsetting them by saying you are not interested in how they feel, but only want the name of the person who angered them? Are they facing you with their arms crossed in a very defensive position? Do you find they are having problems answering your questions and are avoiding any effort you have extended to focus on the key issues? Do they refuse to look you in the face when talking with them?

Monitor what is going on during the interaction so you can take some extra steps to make the relationship a more positive one. These steps may include (1) speaking more slowly, (2) allowing the customer extra time to express frustrations with you, (3) saying several times that you understand, (4) repeating problems for further clarification, or if requested, (5) calling other family members to further explain issues caregivers may not understand.

In a very problematic situation, another option for pleasing the customer is to ask him if he would prefer to work with someone else. Transferring such a relationship to a colleague may be what the customer would like.

Reviewing Customer Relationships

Make a list of four customers who irritate you the most.

For each customer, identify what annoys you.

If you could transfer each one of these relationships/customers to another employee, who would it be and why?

Service cannot be sold as an item or as a packaged product.

While you cannot distribute customer service samples in a box or give them as a gift, the service you deliver is a powerful expression of caring. The service issue is significant enough to be the most talked about topic at your company. It is often the main source of conversation when one customer talks with others about their experiences with your company, and a discussion point at meetings and conferences when professionals share their experiences regarding your particular organization. Nothing is louder than an angry customer just waiting for some ears willing to listen to her rage.

Poor service can be as destructive to any business as any other failing in an organization. While your system for keeping appointments may be computerized and controlled, your attitude and anger may need the same structure. People are apt to speak more about your bad service than they would about a nurse who did not arrive at their home at a prearranged time, a late delivery, or a problem with a particular product. It often takes years to build an outstanding customer service reputation, yet it can be destroyed by one negative comment delivered to one or more key customers in your market. Don't ever sabotage your business relationships with comments like these:

"We have been in the health care business a long time so we have heard it all."

"Why do you think you know more than we do?"

"You would be stupid to call anyone else since we are the best."

"You can do what you want, but you'll call back."

"See if I care!"

Any of these comments can ensure that the customer will not call back.

When we refer to the possibility of poor customer service destroying a company or organization, we are referring to an image that becomes distorted or even destroyed by years of bad press and negative comments. If only in a few short moments you could paint a new picture or create a new aura for your company. Repairing a problem does not happen quickly. While you may have some problems defining and outlining quality service, the customer sees and senses its existence at every point in his involvement with you and your company.

Since service cannot be recalled, apologies are usually the only means of recourse.

Say you are sorry when the customer believes you have made a mistake. Remember that it is appearance that counts, not the reality of the situation. The deed as interpreted by the customer has been done and the memory lingers far longer than you would have ever expected. You cannot set the clock back to a time before the customer became angry so you need to move ahead with a plan for saying you're sorry.

You cannot take back an image, a gesture, or a comment. If the customer believes a certain situation or confrontation happened, you need to go with their reality of what they believe appears to have happened. This must move you to quickly proceed to solving the problem and initiating an apology. You need to begin the process of winning the customer back.

Customers are somewhat like elephants—they never forget. Their anger sometimes lasts longer than their memory of what actually caused them to be upset. Can you recall a customer who told you she would never buy from you again and that this was the end of your relationship? It would be interesting to see if you can go back into your records and files and see if the customer ever called again. Probably not.

The choices among health care providers, insurance companies, physicians, home care companies, and rehabilitation centers are almost endless. The customer who promises never to purchase products or services from you again has many options. Other companies want the business. Many of your competitors are just waiting for you to have a service problem so they can capitalize on your disregard for the value of the customer. For this reason, doing it right the first time is extremely important. You may not be given another opportunity to correct a situation and retain the business and the customer!

Your competitors have ears. They will quickly hear about how you handled a problem or an angry customer. They look for an opportunity to stake their claim to some of the business you may have previously taken away from them. These may be patients, clients, contracts, or alliances they have been wanting for years to acquire.

The manner in which you handle problems can be the deciding factor in the longevity of your relationships with case managers, physician's office staff, insurance company personnel, or others. Plan ahead and work toward avoiding all possible business problems. Try completing a master list of potential problems along with solutions to the problems should they occur. Crisis planning will serve you well.

Problem Apology Checklist

Identify three problems you are now having with customers and the name of the customers.

- Problem _____

  Customer _____

- Problem _____

  Customer _____

- Problem _____

  Customer _____

- Is it possible that you or your company caused these problems?

- If you answered yes, would an apology improve the situation?

- Should you call to apologize? Develop a list of calls you will make today.

Quality service can be a subjective issue.

Yes, take it personally. Customer service is a personal issue. Knowing that the quality of your service will be observed and interpreted by each customer in a different way means you must treat all customers in a manner that meets their particular needs and personalities. With some customers you may need to talk more clearly, while others may need information repeated in several different ways. For example, patients with failing eyesight may need their next appointment written on a large piece of paper or their patient instructions highlighted on the form they are provided. Many patients may find it best to have early morning appointments because of transportation problems. Some case managers or doctors would prefer that you use their private telephone lines or call at a specific time of the day. Frequently customers need constant reminders about appointments or about taking their medications. Knowing and adhering to these special personal customer requests can make all the difference in your business.

Can you recall a colleague who had little or no understanding of insurance policies. You may have met case managers who have never arranged for oxygen or nursing care for home health patients. For many of our colleagues and customers we will need to do just a little more. You may be requested to take those extra steps and do extra things for special people.

Special Customers and Their Special Needs

Make a list of four customers who receive special attention from you or your colleagues and identify why they receive this special treatment?

1. _____

2. _____

3. _____

4. _____

Identify what you did for them that you may not do for others.

What are the three activities or tasks you will do for special customers?

(1) _____ (2) _____ (3) _____

Evaluate this list and explain how these actions may have contributed to your reputation.

Every customer has his own expectations of your organization. For this reason you must determine what the customer needs, and then decide if you are capable of meeting these needs. Knowing what the customer expects and then providing it will be key to developing positive rapport. In order to keep your present business and make new customers happy, you need to offer "diff'rent strokes for diff'rent folks."

For example, the customer who prefers that you fax the contract rather than e-mail it will require extra steps to the fax machine. For the client who needs more explanation of the terms in the policy, you will need to send a glossary of frequently used terms. And for the home care patient who wants the nurse to come after her husband comes home from work, you may find it necessary to alter the nurse's appointment schedule. A service plan developed for the general population that does not allow for customization will not serve you well.

The more people customers must encounter during the order and delivery of any service or product, the less likely they will be satisfied with the service.

You may have heard the request to "keep it simple." Streamlining your operation is more important than ever when it comes to providing quality customer service. Attempt to solve as many of the customer's problems and meet these needs with as few people as possible and in the shortest amount of time. Do all you can to avoid having the customer make numerous calls to your company asking the same question to different people.

Have you ever called a physician's office and had your call passed around to two or three people before they located the person who could schedule the X-ray? The person taking your medical equipment order may not be the person who does the billing, schedules the maintenance, or makes the delivery. The list of specialists involved in the delivery of the service continues to grow. Everyone is a specialist. As more people become involved in the process, so does the possibility the customer will experience service problems.

The more personalities and departments the customer must deal with, the greater the chances that something will go wrong. You can use these customer service strategies to gain your customers' trust and respect:

- Develop fewer lines of communications for the customers. Let them know who to call for what problems and provide direct lines to special people. Let the customers know who is handling their accounts and who can readily access information about them and their needs.

- Avoid having the customers repeat basic billing and delivery information to more than one person. Develop a system or plan where the customers need only speak with one, or no more than two, company representatives regarding any request.

Customers want to speak to the same person all of the time. How can you make that happen in your work setting? Can you streamline the number of contacts your customers must make?

Evaluating Customer Contacts

- Do you have the ability to handle most of the customer requests that come your way?

- Do customers frequently have to talk to more than one person before reaching you? How can this be avoided?

- How often do you find you need to refer the customer to another company representative because you were unable to help them?
  _____ Never   _____ Sometimes   _____ Always

- How often do calls come to you by mistake, where a receptionist/colleague wanted to move the call along and may have had no idea of how to help the customer?
  _____ Never   _____ Rarely   _____ Often   _____ Always

- What steps can your company take to reduce the number of people customers have to deal with?

- What program can be developed to make sure that all the people in the company know the responsibilities of their colleagues?

Review Questions

1. When is service produced?

   _____

   _____

   _____

   _____

2. What determines how a customer will view the service that you provide?

   _____

   _____

   _____

   _____

3. Name behaviors that can help create a positive interaction with a customer.

   _____

   _____

   _____

   _____

4. What should you do if a customer is angry because he believes you made a mistake?

   _____

   _____

   _____

   _____

5. How do you keep service delivery simple?

   _____

   _____

   _____

4

Taking Down the Seven Barriers to Outstanding Customer Service

Objectives

- Identify obstacles in your business operations.

- Understand why it is important to have a system for coordinating customer services.

- Evaluate the impact of employee indifference.

When customer service breaks down and you are no longer fulfilling customer expectations, you will need to audit your entire operation. The only way to solve a problem is to identify its root cause. As you review the barriers to outstanding service described in this chapter, you should find the sources of customer service roadblocks that you are experiencing in your own organization. The exercises are designed to help you evaluate your business practices.

Barrier #1—Policies that exist for the control and convenience of the organization

Too often operating procedures are developed to make the business easier to manage, without much thought for how the procedures will affect the customer. For example, it may be easier for you to make appointments only at certain times of the day or on certain days. Some companies are committed to maintaining structured office hours and avoiding all weekend work, even if their schedule is inconvenient for many of their customers.

Keeping things running smoothly is vital, but it is also important to remain flexible. Policies should be written and enacted to meet the needs of your customers in the most efficient manner possible. When it becomes apparent that policies no longer serve that function, these practices should be reviewed and evaluated in light of the present marketplace.

Never hesitate to change a policy that is no longer serving the best interest of your customers or your operations. A policy should be a win/win situation for both. The purpose is not to keep employees in line, but to ensure quality service that will contribute to the success of the organization.

Evaluating Company Policies

List three company policies that need immediate evaluation, change, or elimination.

1. _____

2. _____

3. _____

Barrier #2—Failure to coordinate services

Sometimes it takes more than one person to provide a service or product for the customer, so it is important to establish a system for coordinating information. One person may take the request for insurance information, another then places the brochure in an envelope for mailing, and a third person comes by to pick it up. Coordinating company services may require: (1) developing special checklists; (2) recording important times and dates; and (3) holding meetings to review, discuss, and evaluate how all services should be coordinated. Everyone needs to know who will do what, when, and for whom.

Knowing that most of your services or products must pass through several sets of hands before reaching the customer requires you to pay full attention to the coordination of all the details to ensure that the customer receives what they expect. For example, people who market your products may be making promises regarding the delivery of a product with little understanding of how it all happens.

Who Promises for You?

What are two promises others have made that you were unable to make good?

1. _____

2. _____

Who are the people who make promises for you?

In retrospect what would you now like to tell the people who made these promises?

(Careful what you're thinking!)

Everyone must understand what they need to do and what roles other team members will play. You must develop a well-oiled system. One member of your team cannot handle it alone. Just look around and you learn that rather quickly. You must be able to trust others in your organization to follow up on requests that you make of them, since others are relying on you to keep the promises that you make. We must have a circle of trust within our own organization if the customer is to be totally satisfied.

Barrier #3—Decision makers who have had little contact with customers

Customers need to interact with people who have the power to help them. Many employees are not empowered to make decisions and must constantly ask others for approval for almost every decision they make. Waiting for someone else—who may be the only person authorized to answer a question—can be irritating and frustrating. Yes, some questions will always require management decisions. But too frequently the person speaking with the customer seems to be "just working there" and is unable to offer answers. Understand your powers as an employee or manager and how you can speed the customer to the solution of his/her problems. You may need to have a special meeting with management to discuss this issue. What are your job responsibilities?

Another frustrating situation can occur when management and key decision makers have not spoken to a customer in many months or even years. You may wish that they had a better understanding of your customers, the order fulfillment process, or key accounts. Too bad you cannot secretly send them a letter notifying them it is time to get out of their offices and meet with customers up close and personal.

Waiting for someone else to help your customer creates customer frustration and failure to develop a customer commitment. Work with management in addressing this situation. Discuss the issue with your colleagues, managers, and supervisors.

Your Decision-Making Powers

- What are the decisions I am able to make?
- Who are the key decision makers I need to turn to about particular issues that arise during my interactions with customers?
- Identify the key issues and the person who handles the particular problem:

The issue _____ The decision maker _____

The issue _____ The decision maker _____

The issue _____ The decision maker _____

- What are the limits of my powers or areas I cannot address with my customers?
- How can I become better informed about my organization and my own decision-making areas?

Barrier #4—When the top priority is cost containment

Sacrificing quality service for the sake of increasing profits is a mistake. If you continue to place profits above service, you will lose. Your sole priority should not be reducing costs. You will find yourself giving up the value-added services that may cost extra dollars but could be a main reason you have come to enjoy a reasonable amount of business success.

Your business priorities should be multifocused, with **cost-containment** being only one of them. Saving money should never be your overriding mission. If you are concerned about spending those extra dollars mailing a report for next-day delivery, think again. This step could be the one extra service that separates you from the competition. If you have decided to save money by reducing the number of people answering your telephones, you may want to reconsider. Lost calls ultimately mean lost business. The drive to reduce costs often leads a company to cut back on intangible services that are important for holding its place in the industry.

Cost-Containment Efforts

Identify two cost-containment efforts enacted in your company that may have caused you to lose customers:

1. _____

2. _____

How could these situations have been avoided?

_____

In an age of networks, alliances, and partnerships, companies need to learn when to walk away from business deals that could seriously damage their reputation and the public image that they have worked hard to establish. If reducing cost is your primary reason for joining forces with another organization, think again. You need to have a shared mission with a business partner and a mutual belief in the factors that actually help build a profitable business.

Barrier #5—Indifferent and unmotivated employees

Customer service suffers when just one employee does not care. As an employee, you must evaluate your own commitment to the organization and determine if you are in the right place. Your behavior and attitude affect everyone you work with and work for. Although you may have respect for the company, you may see yourself as being better suited for another position in the organization.

One person not committed to providing great customer service can be devastating to the organization. For example, being careful about scheduling an appointment for a client does not mean the receptionist will show the same concern when the person shows up and waits more than an hour to see you or your boss. Calling the customer back to verify that you have in stock the item they requested does not mean that the warehouse manager can guarantee delivery as promised.

If you are noticing a change in your own commitment, it may be time for a conversation with your manager. You may want to talk with the appropriate person about your own level of frustration or unhappiness with the organization. You may want to offer, always in a tactful manner, suggestions for improving the work environment. These may include more staff meetings, opportunities to meet with managers and express opinions about protocols that may affect your work. And in the same careful manner, express feelings about how operations can be improved and how everyone can be encouraged to remember the importance of the customer. Keep in mind, while management may listen to you, they will not necessarily act and make immediate changes. Be patient. You may have to voice the same message several times in various ways before your suggestions are fully digested.

As for **self-evaluation,** catch the problem of your own indifference and lack of motivation before it affects both the organization and you personally. Take your own inventory concerning your feelings about work. It may be the right time to begin looking for employment somewhere else. Have you given this a thought?

Barrier #6—Failure to listen and learn from colleagues

If you are committed to improving customer service, start listening and learning from other employees. Often the best advice regarding what a customer needs or wants comes from coworkers. Our colleagues become our best trainers. Talking to your colleagues, sharing ideas and suggestions should become a part of company training and education programs.

People bring outstanding past experiences to their positions. They are often eager to share operational skills that worked well at their previous place of employment. We should learn about customer service strategies that made a difference at other companies and model some of these behaviors. Everyone wants to hear about ideas that have been tested and proven to work. Our colleagues bring with them experiences from their personal lives and from their dealings with other businesses. Tapping into an employee's long-term work experiences can be an important educational resource. Planning issue-oriented meetings with fellow employees to discuss this can be valuable in enhancing the quality of your operation.

What Have You Learned from Working Elsewhere?

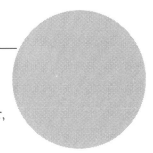

- What have you learned from previous employers that would work at your new job?

- Is there a customer service strategy that did not work at your previous employer, but might work well now?

Barrier #7—The impression that customer service is a job responsibility for only a select few employees

Customer service must not be described as the job responsibility for only a few select employees. Too many employees believe the customer service function is a separate entity from contracting, accounting, case management, billing, marketing, or clinical services. This is a serious misconception.

Customer service is an organizational responsibility, not a job description. It calls for a philosophy that permeates all areas of the organization. To keep customer service front and center, you must:

- discuss customer service issues at all department meetings,

- monitor and review problems and trends, and

- constantly survey customers and measure outcomes.

The subject must be included as a part of all staff development programs. If customer service ever becomes a task for only a limited number of employees, then it will be delivered to only a limited number of customers.

In addition to the seven barriers we just discussed, other obstacles can prevent companies from earning high marks from customers, including:

- Not taking the time to define the standards you need to achieve. Standards help guide everyone's interactions with customers.

- Focusing on new technology as a means for improving service, rather than on the people who interact with customers. Customer service is a people business, and technology can never replace the value of human interactions. Technology is a support system used to enhance the customer service operation—not replace it!

- Not developing management skills and leadership capable of guiding decisions to ensure that customers receive what they need. Leaders must keep the organization focused on the provision of quality service, developing both internal and external customer improvement programs and monitors.

- Placing customer service issues in a file for addressing at some other time. Companies that do this will self-destruct.

- Failing to study and evaluate the marketplace on a regular basis. Gathering data allows the company to set standards based on scientific research, and to track and analyze industry trends.

- Misjudging the power and impact of the customer, both as a revenue source and public relations agent.

Customer Service Barriers

List and describe five barriers to quality service that exist in your company.

1. _____

2. _____

3. _____

4. _____

5. _____

Review Questions

1. What is the best way to handle a policy that is having a negative effect on customer relations?

   _____

   _____

   _____

   _____

2. Why is it important to empower employees to make decisions involving the customer?

   _____

   _____

   _____

   _____

3. What can we learn from the work experience of colleagues?

   _____

   _____

   _____

   _____

4. Name three ways you can gain support for outstanding service.

   _____

   _____

   _____

   _____

5. How should you make suggestions for improving operations?

   _____

   _____

   _____

   _____

5

Strategies for Delivering Quality Service

Objectives

- Describe the impact of the first interaction with the customer.

- Learn effective customer service strategies.

- Know the most important questions to ask customers.

- Recognize the difference between perception and reality in the mind of the customer.

Delivering quality service has become an art form. It has different shades, perspectives, and feelings. It is created with a great deal of thought, planning, and consideration of the recipient. And it takes constant reminders and dedication on the part of every member of your organization.

Your service is one of the primary reasons customers prefer to do business with you. Customers who return obviously like the service they have received and want more of the same. They also tell their friends and colleagues what to expect when they deal with you. Outstanding service is one way to create customer loyalty.

With the growing competition in the health care industry, the service you provide may be the one ingredient that sets you apart from others in the industry. Customers are always trying to determine who offers the best service. Professional referral sources are constantly challenged to select the very best provider for their clients; and with so many companies vying for their attention, the decision is difficult. Service is clearly an attribute that can generate positive feelings and draw customers to your business.

Most case managers, physicians, nurses, and social workers, as well as patients select health care providers without first visiting their business location or observing their operation. The service you provide becomes the window to your operation. Make your first contact inviting because it will influence how the customer judges your entire organization. The initial service—your greeting and your willingness to help—may be what persuades the customer to begin the relationship.

Your business is often judged by one encounter with the customer. A brief telephone call could push the customer in one direction or another. After one contact, the customer begins to question whether she should take the risk of calling you again. Should I continue coming here for my treatment? Will they be helpful in a crisis? Can they be easily reached when I have a question? The decision is a personal one and may be based on one positive or negative interaction with staff. This interaction may be with only one person in the organization. It is also interesting to see how quickly business relationships can take some interesting turns.

As you continue to explore the impact of good service, reflect upon your personal experiences with other businesses. What did other companies do that impressed you? What was said to you as a customer that made you like the company you were doing business with? Why do you continually shop in certain stores or eat in selected restaurants? Did they do something special that made them stand apart from their competitors?

Service That Impressed You

Identify two stores, restaurants, or physician's offices you went to during the past year and what impressed you.

1. _____

2. _____

Think about the attitude and presentation skills of those who offered to help you. Ask yourself the following questions:

- Did they act like you were an annoyance?

- Did their staff act as if you were taking up some of their precious time?

- Did they make you feel that the time they were devoting to you could have been dedicated to more important tasks or even more important people?

Your observations will make you keenly aware of the kind of service you should be providing.

Analyze Service You Did Not Like

Identify two stores, restaurants, or offices where you were provided poor service and probably will not return. Do you recall why?

1. _____ Why? _____

2. _____ Why? _____

Once you have the customer in the door, what's next? How can you keep him coming back? For starters, you can begin by reviewing and practicing these 13 strategies for better performance.

Strategy #1—Know what the customer wants.

You cannot provide quality service unless you first determine the special needs of your customer. This process may take more time than you expect, but the end result will be worth all of your efforts. It will involve asking many questions. Make a list of what you need to know and the questions you must ask. You may need to verify information that you didn't hear clearly or do follow-up research on a particular disease state. Since your goal is to provide the services and products the customer wants and expects, you must gather and understand all the relevant facts concerning your customer.

Your Most Important Questions

What five questions do you have to ask almost every new customer?

1. _____

2. _____

3. _____

4. _____

5. _____

You must understand the marketplace in which you are transacting business. What are the services and products offered by your competitors? You can often learn what the customer wants by determining what they have received from your competition. You need to track the products that are most widely known to your customers and those that are continually requested by referral sources. You must also understand the types of requests made by specific customer groups (for example, the elderly, the physically challenged, case managers, physicians).

What Do Health Care Customers Want to Know?

What are the five most frequent questions customers ask when calling your office?
Are you ready to answer them?

1. Question _____ Yes ___ No ___

2. Question _____ Yes ___ No ___

3. Question _____ Yes ___ No ___

4. Question _____ Yes ___ No ___

5. Question _____ Yes ___ No ___

If there were lots of *no's* in your response, you may have homework to do. When you wear the customer service hat, which everyone in your company should be wearing, you must continue to ask: "How may I help you?" and "What other information can I provide?" Are you aware of a service or product you provide, but whose description or benefits you are not familiar with? You cannot provide quality service without a full understanding of all that your company offers. You can imagine how frustrating it is for a customer to call your company only to discover that the customer service representative is not sure which products the company sells or even the schedule of office hours on a particular day. Since good customer service requires you to become a "customer educator," you must first educate yourself.

Most Frequently Asked Questions

Identify five questions customers have the most difficulty answering? Is there a way you can help them locate the answers?

1. _____

2. _____

3. _____

4. _____

5. _____

To understand and catalog some of the unique needs of particular types of customers, it is a good idea to prepare an **account assessment** for each customer. The account assessment is a record of customer characteristics and buying patterns that is easily accessible and updated on a regular basis. Your account assessment should include but not be limited to: (1) complete contact information, (2) organizational chart indicating where the person you are dealing with fits into the organization, (3) any of his special needs, (4) a list of all the services and products provided, (5) who to contact when the customer cannot be reached, (6) problems the customer may have had with other health care providers/businesses, (7) what service issues are most important to the customer, and (8) how and best times to contact them (for example, fax, e-mail, or telephone).

Strategy #2—Create a service state of mind.

When you are at work, customer service must become a state of mind. It needs to be thought about at the moment you open the store, enter the office, pick up the telephone, respond to a customer request, provide reimbursement information, meet with a referral source, make a delivery, or initiate a conversation. It is a feeling or atmosphere conveyed throughout the organization. Some customers will have problems describing exactly how you offer outstanding service. They may perceive it as an "indescribable" condition. People often have problems explaining something intangible. Service is so basic—like being polite, listening to the customer, and showing respect for others. It has to do with personal character traits, the ability to show sincere concern and responsiveness. It must be graciously and effortlessly offered by someone who is able to attend to needs beyond her own.

Your goal is to create a special feeling between provider and customer. It happens as soon as you hear each other's voice and will become evident as you begin to interact. When you are tired and must repeat the same information over and over, you are put to the test. Quality service is never lax. If the customer asks you to again fax the authorization or resend materials that you know you already sent, you find yourself controlling your negative comments and doing what was requested. You come to the realization that in the name of quality customer service, you may need to perform the very same task more than once.

It all has to do with patience, a trait synonymous with quality service. You want the customer to like you and your business. Have you ever repeated your telephone number or your name several times and wondered if the customer is listening? Have you ever faxed the same report twice in the same day knowing you sent it to the number provided you and you feel certain the receiver misplaced the document? If you have, you just have to keep thinking, this is all part of the job and there is more to win by trying to make the customer happy than by ceasing to be cooperative.

You cannot hesitate as you deliver quality service. Quality service must become a natural activity, the comfortable and right thing to do. It must become a part of all your office interactions. Practice with your colleagues so the behaviors become even more natural. The fastest way to practice is to begin providing this same level of service to those you work with. When you treat your colleagues as customers, the practice becomes routine. Eventually it will permeate your entire workday. If being polite causes any hesitation, then more training and practice are needed. Some organizations actually promote a two-tiered culture. For example, calls coming from inside the office are answered one way; calls coming from outside are answered another way. Is there a difference in how the telephone is answered in your office?

Strategy #3—Practice active listening.

Quality customer service means listening carefully and paying attention to what is being said. Make sure you understand what is requested and let the customer know that you understand. You cannot respond to customer needs if you do not know what they are. When listening to someone standing in front of you, make eye contact, nod your head, or verbally acknowledge what was said. You need to listen attentively, not merely wait to enter the conversation. Let the customer know you are listening. When talking on the telephone, be an equal partner in the conversation. With words like, "Yes, I understand" and "OK," you become a participant in the interaction. You are letting the customer know you are focused on what he is saying and actively listening to him.

It is best to avoid distractions when listening. Listening takes concentration and distractions make it more difficult. Most of us have had the experience with telephone calls that after you said goodbye and reviewed the conversation, you realized you weren't listening as well as you thought you were. Take a moment to hold your calls, close your door, and, if it works for you, clear your desk before you speak to a customer about important issues.

Customers need and require your full and undivided attention. If you are ever going to understand the intricacies of their particular medical or insurance situation, you need to listen. No matter how much experience you've had in your area of expertise, there is something to learn from each person. Never believe you have heard or seen it all. Listening will be one of your best techniques for understanding the customer.

Check Your Listening Techniques

1. Do you look directly at your customers when they are in front of you?

2. Are you aware of their body language and their choice of words?

3. Does your mind wander during some conversations?

4. Do you make your customer nervous by your position or authority?

5. Do you find some customers do not listen to your suggestions?

6. Do you listen for the uniqueness of each customer's issue?

Strategy #4—Question the customer to get a fuller understanding of his needs.

With the intent of providing outstanding customer service, listening may not be enough. Many times when you hear something said, the exact meaning may not be clear. People use words in different ways. Each segment of the industry has its own terminology. Many of the words we use everyday may be unfamiliar to people sitting in the room just across the hall. Even within your own department, certain terms may need clarification if anyone outside the office is to understand what you are referring to.

Terms That Cause Customer Service Problems

What terms do you use that customers/clients frequently misunderstand? What terms need to be clarified and explained? List them:

1. _____   4. _____

2. _____   5. _____

3. _____   6. _____

Consider developing a glossary of frequently used terms that can be shared with your colleagues. It may also be useful to create another glossary of terms that can be shared with your customers.

How to create a glossary for your office

Follow these steps in creating a glossary of terms for your customers:

1. Ask all members of your office to submit a list of terms they want included.

2. Ask several key people to write definitions of these terms.

3. Select definitions that are clear and easy to understand.

4. Distribute the glossary to patients, referral sources, receptionists, and new and experienced employees.

5. On an annual basis review the glossary and add terms that are new and most frequently questioned.

Many times you think you know what the patient is expecting simply because you have heard all the words she spoke. This may not be true. While the words may be clear, the interpretations may be different. While the customer may have heard you say the word *immediately*, it may take on a different connotation than you intended. The only way you can be sure that everyone has the same understanding is to ask for clarification, explanation, and agreement.

Never be ashamed to ask for words or comments to be explained in more detail. You must question all issues that are not clear to you. Ask about items that you don't understand, products you may be unfamiliar with, or confusing billing issues. Surprisingly customers often hear about your new product or policy before the entire staff is informed. While it may be embarrassing when this happens, you need to be willing to do your homework so you can provide correct and complete information. You may need clarification about the time a patient was admitted to a hospital, discharged from the clinic, about a diagnosis, the number of the group insurance policy, the name of the employer, or how physically able the patient is to resume daily activities. Ask whatever you need to know. You can only be refused information.

You may find you need more extensive mailing instructions, alternate fax numbers, or travel directions in order to make a timely delivery of a medical product. It is vitally important for you to ask any questions about anything you do not understand. Listen carefully since you want to get all the information correct the first time. You also may not be able to obtain accurate information the first time since important information may have been omitted. You may need to again call back, although hopefully this can be avoided. Customers are often very unforgiving, so getting it right the first time is so important. Remember, the competition is waiting for you to make that first mistake so it can capture business created by your poor service. Your mistakes can be your competitor's good fortune!

Everyone you do business with wants to be clearly understood. They want things to happen as they understand and expect them to. They want you as an insurance provider or health care manager to let them know if they cannot expect the service to happen as it was promised or as they have come to expect it. With insurance, customers usually purchase the product at a time when they probably have no immediate plans to use it. Therefore, they examine the policy in a very different way than if they were to use it immediately. Our customers may not know enough to ask the right questions at the time of the purchase. So you must listen carefully to find out if there are gaps in the customer's knowledge.

Ask for clarification of any issue that you feel is not clear to your customer. Also ask about information you have received that is not clear to you. It is far more important to have all the correct information, than to simply "get it done" so you can move on to the next telephone call or meeting. The angry customer can become your most disastrous nightmare.

Strategy #5—Envision the health care customer as a profit center.

Customers must become your business partners. They can help you make or lose money. They are drawn to your business for a myriad reasons, and they are capable of making important financial decisions that can affect your business.

While it is true people have various reasons for pursuing their business goals, money is often one of the prime motivators. If ensuring the viability of a profitable organization is one of your key motivators, then it is important to view each customer as a **profit center**. You need to track and monitor the business they generate. Every customer comes to your organization with the possibility of spending money. These customers may be advisors to other business operations, associates, or patients who may be considering spending their own health care dollars with you or with an organization similar to yours.

With every customer you speak to or meet with, you need to understand that much of the money generated from this contact is returned to you in salary, company benefits, and future business. His investment in your company allows you to pay your mortgage, drive your car, feed your family, or take a vacation. If you recognize the customer as a profit center with the potential for creating ongoing revenues, you should have no problem focusing on service.

Now you can see how to equate good service with increased profits. After reviewing the account records of many health care organizations you notice a tremendous amount of repeat business. Companies are profitable because customers keep coming back again and again. These organizations quickly become leaders in the industry. You need to talk with your own repeat customers and find out what is important to them.

Strategy # 6—Make the customer feel important.

Everyone you do business with wants to feel that she is your most important customer. She *is* important and needs to know that you recognize that. The key is to know how to make her feel important. She helped you build your business, maintain your reputation, feed your family, and pay your bills. She is an excellent source for spreading the word about your outstanding work. She is more apt to talk positively about you once she knows how much you value her business. Your plan is to find ways to let her know you are aware of her importance. Here are suggestions for sharing this information.

- Send a thank-you note for all new business.

- Close telephone conversations with a message about how much you appreciate their call.

- Call to thank any person who has referred business to you.

- Tell customers they are important to your business and how much you value the business relationship.

To do this you will need to give the customer your undivided attention and schedule some uninterrupted time. This may require you to turn off your cell phones, close your door, and stop saying "my door is always open." If your door is always open, you may be unable to get anything done. You cannot effectively handle more than one customer service issue at a time.

Nothing can be more powerful than telling the customer that he is important to your business. Remember, it is your long-term business contacts and customer trust in what you do that allows you to continue to succeed in business. You have made your customers feel valued and in return they have given you their loyalty. Encourage the feeling.

Make your customers feel as though you not only want their business, but you want to keep their business. Make sure that if the customers were ever to talk about you to anyone else, they would have nothing but wonderful remarks to make about your company.

Letting Customers Know They Are Important

What do you do to let customers know they are important to your business?

1. _____

2. _____

3. _____

Strategy #7—Back your business with honesty.

Have you ever lied to a customer? Have you ever told customers that you have the information they need, only to find that you are going to have to do some additional research to locate it? Have you ever told customers that the person he was calling was in the office, and then realized that he was out at an appointment? Have you ever promised the customer that you will mail a report, only to find that you were unable to prepare the materials requested in a timely manner? In the eyes of the customer you may not have been as honest as you intended. While lying would be a rather forceful word to describe your actions, that may be the word the customer is using to talk about the incident to someone else.

Your business cannot survive without treating all customers with honesty. It is an element in the customer service process that must become a part of every interaction. Realizing you are in business to stay in business makes the honesty issue more important. Honesty is the insurance policy that you provide to your customers to ensure the long-term prosperity of your organization. Trust in each other is the basis for successful business relationships: Trust that you will call back when you have promised, keep appointments as scheduled, and give the customers complete and honest information about what they are buying.

Through your interactions with a customer you realize your own career and reputation is at stake. When you forfeit honesty for the sake of short-term profits or a "quick-hit," everyone loses—especially you. The one thing you will take with you whenever you decide to leave the organization will be your reputation. Protect it at all times. You have spent years cultivating and developing a good reputation. You cannot afford to see it destroyed by inappropriate comments to a customer or an unchecked promise to a colleague.

A company that embraces ethical and honest behavior, and lives by that creed, goes a long way toward ensuring long-term success for itself. Your outstanding personal ethical reputation will enhance the image of your company and be a formidable reason for people to do business with you. Honesty is a core value of quality customer service in the health care industry.

Strategy #8—Keep your promises.

A key to good customer service is your commitment to keep the promises you make. Often in your efforts to obtain the business and to capture new accounts from the competition, you will find yourself making promises that you cannot keep. Promising actions or products that you cannot deliver as requested may be your downfall. When you promise that a colleague will deliver a report to a particular office without verifying that it can be done, you may be making a promise you cannot keep. This is a very sensitive issue, since the customer or referral source will be waiting to see how well you keep your promises and may use this to separate you from the competition.

When you promise that you or a representative of your company will return a call to a patient/client or be at a meeting at a particular time, can you be sure that this will happen? Have you first spoken to the office manager, nursing director, delivery person, or store manager before making a promise to the customer? Are you sure your colleagues are able to keep the promises you make to customers on their behalf? For example, if you have indicated to a customer that Medicare or their insurance will not pay for a particular service or product, have you verified this with the latest guidelines?

Make sure you have done the appropriate research before you make any promises. Avoid being trapped in situations you cannot handle. Do not allow your customers to turn your failed promises into lies, or give them unwarranted excuses for taking their business to your competitor.

Broken promises may be the cause for not only losing business, but for destroying your reputation. Your customer service is always being scrutinized. Judging your service by the promises you keep is an easy test for customers to perform. Too often we quickly make a promise that we pay little attention to. We never think the promise may be the test that allows the customer a quick assessment of whether we can be trusted to do what we say.

Promises must go along with a behavior—as answers must match questions. When the answers do not happen, you lose. When enough answers do not match, you will be out of the game. How many promises do you need to break before you lose the business? Often, only ONE! Your company, and you as a representative of the organization, should never be taking those chances. Have you recently made a promise for someone else only to find that he or she was unable to keep it?

Strategy #9—Offer to help your customer.

Great customer service means helping the customer. You help by assisting the customer in locating what she needs, either in terms of the services or products you offer, or by helping her find what she needs somewhere else in the health care environment. You help when you meet customers' needs and their customer service expectations—with a minimum of stress and anxiety. You can also help the customer understand some of the confusing aspects of the health care system and the effects of reimbursement regulations on the purchase and costs of the products or services he wishes to obtain. You can help in many ways.

Helping is a willingness to do the very best you can to meet customers' needs and to maintain their loyalty. At your company you need to become more than a service provider or sales representative. You must become a health care consultant to your customers. Try the proactive approach—by anticipating needs and offering to help the customer even before they ask.

Strategy #10—Express gratitude for the business.

Customers are often confused and frustrated. Sometimes they are unsure of what they need. Perhaps they were referred to you by a third party and they are not familiar with the services you provide. They have your business card and remember being told that you would be the person to help them. They often do not understand many of the questions you ask or issues you refer to.

What everyone needs to understand is that customers have choices. Knowing they could be taking their questions to any on your long list of competitors, you must be appreciative of their business. You must not only show appreciation for this first visit or call, but you should begin working toward developing a long-term relationship built on trust and rapport. You have been blessed that this customer has taken the chance and given you the opportunity to serve her. And for some, it is a chance and a risk she may not be sure about. She may know little about your products and be unfamiliar with the services you offer. Knowing this makes it very important to express your gratitude to the customer for taking this risk and entrusting you with her business.

Your gratitude can be expressed through a variety of activities or behaviors. It can be shown through (1) a written thank-you note, (2) a personal call, (3) a letter, or (4) for even greater impact, a personal meeting to express appreciation. The meeting can be made by you or by another supervisor or manager at your company. A personal meeting with a company manager may be especially valuable when you are receiving this business from another professional colleague. No matter what approach you select to show your appreciation, do it with sincerity, always letting the customers know how much you appreciate their business.

A Customer Gratitude Check

Do you have any thank-you notes in your office?

When did you last write a letter or thank-you note?

If you were to write thank-you notes, who are the first five people you would write to and what would you thank them for?

1. _____

2. _____

3. _____

4. _____

5. _____

Strategy #11—Show your customer courtesy.

Talking to fellow employees, your colleagues, or supervisors about courtesy can be a very difficult and sensitive task. People are usually very defensive when engaged in a discussion about their own behavior. They often quickly defend themselves against any attack regarding what may be seen as rude or uncomplimentary actions. We often find excuses for our own negative behaviors and sometimes deny they happened. Too often, we fail to realize that at times we lose it. We say things that we don't mean and express an attitude that may be unpleasant.

Unfortunately, how we feel on a particular day can affect how we present ourselves to our colleagues as well as to our customers. We must learn to be aware of our image and how others see us. Good customer service has to do with being respectful and polite. It has to do with using some special words we learned as a child like *please* and *thank you*. Often saying these words is not as important as the impact and memory of others who did not say them. Remember, forgetting to thank people for their business is what some customers seem to talk about the most.

Living by the golden rule can have long-term, positive effects on your company. Be polite. It really works as a customer service strategy and will have positive effects on your bottom line. Make polite behavior a part of every approach to the customer. Include it in your customer service philosophy and make it a part of your company mission. Make yours a company people like to do business with and feel secure in referring to their friends and colleagues. Give the respect you wish to receive and expect the same in return from the customers you do business with.

Strategy #12—Admit when you are wrong.

Good customer service often requires apologizing and admitting when you or your company has done something wrong. While you may only appear wrong in the eyes of the customer, what appears to have happened is more important than what actually did. The customer's perception is what counts. You may be technically correct even though the customer believes you are wrong. If this happens, it is time to work on solving this problem of appearing to have made a mistake. If you quoted the customer a wrong price on a product or policy, move quickly to call them back with an apology. Do not wait for him to correct you.

It is the perception of right or wrong that you must deal with now. If the customer feels that the person on the telephone did not take enough interest in their request or showed little concern for ensuring that all would go as planned, you must admit that this perception is valid and accept the responsibility to apologize and correct the situation.

Trying to win a point over the customer can only cause you to lose business. You cannot win. There is nothing to win by proving the customer wrong. Many of your referral sources and customers want to be in control of a situation and having them convince you to admit you were wrong may just be the issue that keeps the business coming back to your company. This may be difficult to accept, but it can prove to be a winning tactic. When was the last time you apologized to a customer, knowing you did not make a mistake?

Something can be learned from every interaction especially when a problem or altercation arises. While you determine how the problem occurred, move on with a rapid and sincere apology. Thank your customer for bringing the issue to your attention and helping you become a more efficient and customer responsive business. The incident may have supplied you with valuable training and education that will allow you to keep some very important customers in the future.

Your Mistakes and Actions

1. What was the last mistake you made with a customer?

2. Did you call or send an apology when you realized you made a mistake?

3. What was the result of your apology?

You are seeking the customer's long-term business so winning a point over a $50 or $100 service/product may not be worth it. You will need to evaluate each individual situation before making this business decision. You do not want to lose business because of unthinking comments or actions. Your goal is to win customers, business, and a good reputation—not an argument. Your best plan of action is to accept responsibility for a mistake. Admitting you're wrong will provide you and your company with the ultimate win, allowing for long-term relationships and profits—not short-term successes.

Strategy #13—Acknowledge your customer's feelings.

While we cannot always walk in the shoes of our customers, we all can do a better job of trying to understand their needs and feelings. Good customer service means being sensitive.

Illness often affects our ability to think clearly and rationally. Patients and families may be upset, in pain, depressed, or frustrated with the medical crisis at hand. The case manager may be having a difficult time locating resources or understanding coverage issues in their client's insurance policy. The consumer may be overwhelmed with her health care experience. You will continually be called on to express and acknowledge your sensitivity to the customer's situation.

The customer may be in a hurry when calling your office or entering your store. He may have reluctantly accepted the role of caregiver. He may have recently assumed the responsibility to direct and monitor the care of a loved one whom he had not seen in many years or possibly he is acting on behalf of a neighbor calling on him to help. You must be sensitive to any number of these stressful situations for customers.

Customers have their good and bad days. Just as you have days that often do not go as planned, so do customers. At an appropriate time, let people know you understand their frustrations and how they feel. Your customers want to know that you understand their anxieties. As an employee in the health care industry you must be sensitive to the pressures a customer may experience when asked to complete a task, wait for a service, or be compelled to purchase a wheelchair she may need for the rest of her life. You must learn to empathize. What would your feelings be if it were you ordering oxygen to use every day for your own survival?

During every interaction you and the customer bring to the relationship a unique blend of feelings, attitudes, stressors, and needs. Customers may not be sure how they feel. You may even find customers quickly rejecting any help that you can offer or advice that you might share. The customer's emotions may be complex, but your acceptance of this full range of human emotions is a valuable ingredient in your mission to develop positive, profitable relationships.

Review Questions

1. How can you determine what your customer needs?

   _____

   _____

   _____

   _____

2. When is the best time to think about customer service?

   _____

   _____

   _____

   _____

3. What is a useful skill for understanding your customer's requests?

   _____

   _____

   _____

   _____

4. How can you make the customer feel important?

   _____

   _____

   _____

   _____

5. How do you benefit personally from the business customers bring to your organization?

   _____

   _____

   _____

   _____

PART TWO

Communicating with Customers

6

Tools for Clear Communication

Objectives

- Understand the effect of language and tone of voice in spoken communications.

- Define the value of clearly understanding the customer's message.

- Know the essential information to provide every customer.

Effective communication is vital for comprehending your customers' needs and establishing what customers can expect from you. Whether the form is oral or written, the participants must clearly understand each other. Keep in mind that people have different styles and preferences in the ways they send and receive information. For example, younger folks may be more comfortable communicating electronically, while seniors may prefer information in writing. The techniques discussed here are key to clear communication—no matter what system you use or demographic you target. You can employ these strategies for all your communications.

Speak in a language the customer will understand.

People who work in the health care industry use abbreviations and terminology developed for their special fields. We often speak with our colleagues in codes only insiders can understand. Technical or professional jargon may not be easily understood by the customer. When we do business with people outside our industry, we may be using terms that are completely unfamiliar to them. People who have had little contact with your industry, products, or services may have no understanding of terms like "indemnity" or "beneficiary." When you use words that are unfamiliar to the customer, you are causing confusion and anxiety.

It is not just external customers that you need to worry about. Don't be fooled into believing that your professional associates understand everything fully. Clinicians may not be familiar with insurance terminology, just as an oncology nurse may not be aware of the newest diabetic treatment programs. And don't assume providers of home medical equipment have had experience with long-term care insurance or that the nursing home administrator understands what services require additional documentation for authorizing payment.

The point is you may need to explain certain issues more than once or clarify instructions. Unclear messages can become a great concern to the customer and lead to more serious complaints. The customer may need more detailed information from you or one of your associates. You may need to break down the cost of premiums, spell out benefits, prepare written instructions for submitting payments, explain how the policy is to be renewed, and provide contact names and telephone numbers for emergency services or your billing department. During every interaction, think first about what you are going to say and then rephrase your message in words the customer will understand.

Encourage the customer to ask questions.

In any exchange with customers, make sure that you're not doing all the talking. Because of anxiety, the customer may have many questions to ask and may need to ask the same question more than once. Do not become annoyed when you have to repeat information.

Customer's Most Frequently Asked Questions and Your Responses

Identify five issues customers ask about most frequently.

1. _____

2. _____

3. _____

4. _____

5. _____

What materials can you (or your company) provide to make it easier for customers to understand the issues they are concerned about?

1. _____

2. _____

3. _____

If you find that the customer is not asking about important issues, be assertive and invite her questions. While she may not feel comfortable asking you about what she does not understand, you may have to encourage her to ask and even give her permission to do so. She may feel somewhat intimidated by your position and knowledge and be reluctant to question your explanations. Let the customer know it is okay to ask questions at any time.

The Difficult Terms

Identify the 10 most difficult terms for customers to understand? How can you provide clarification of these terms?

1. _____   6. _____

2. _____   7. _____

3. _____   8. _____

4. _____   9. _____

5. _____   10. _____

Speak in a tone of voice that indicates assurance.

Make the customer feel that he is doing business with a company that he can trust. Speak clearly and loudly enough for the customer to hear without straining to listen. Speak with confidence about what you will be doing for the customer. Make the customer feel that everything you promise will be done according to agreed upon expectations. The sound and tone of your voice is extremely important in letting the customer know that he is doing business with an organization that understands his need, can meet the need, and is the right company to help him. The deeper tones in your voice will convey a sign of assurance. Speaking with little hesitation will also make the customer more comfortable about his selection of providers. You want him to feel that you are actually going to do what you say you are going to do.

Always ask for understanding.

Never close a discussion with a customer without ensuring that there is complete understanding of what is expected and verifying all necessary information. If you need additional information about the illness, address, family contact information, or payment plan, ask the customer. If you need for the customer to understand certain specific items completely and clearly, verify that he understands.

You do not want the customer (1) to have any unanswered questions or (2) to have misinterpreted any of the information that you have provided. You may need to clarify points about how much a service or item will cost, what payments will be required, what additional insurance information you will need to supply for reimbursement, or the person to call in the evening or on weekends. Never be reluctant to repeat any information. At some point in your life the situation could be reversed and you or a family member could be the customer and you will be a grateful receiver of that extra bit of attention. Never believe that because you think you have given the customer a clear explanation of an issue or program, it has been received with the same clarity. Always check for understanding. It will save you time, energy, and business.

Provide written information about services or products.

To help reduce some of the stress experienced by customers as they deal with a new industry for the first time, it is important to provide written information about your service or product. With new regulations and changing policies, consumers need guidance. You should be there to provide it. They may need information to share with caregivers involved with their treatment, or to further understand their illnesses or the insurance they purchased. People may know what their insurance plans cost but fail to comprehend what they cover. They know there are deductibles but are unclear as to how much and for what products.

Too frequently, information is given to patients during times when they are extremely anxious about any number of issues. They are often not listening carefully. The questions they want to ask may come to them at the close of your conversation or even after the meeting is over. It is helpful to provide additional written information, which will provide your customers with better understanding at a time when it may be easier for them to relax and concentrate. When you develop **customer education materials,** remember the following:

1. Write the materials in a language customers will understand.

2. Have several people outside the industry or your office review the materials before they are produced.

3. Keep the document concise and to the point.

4. Provide important contact information.

Customer Education Materials

Make a list of the written materials you provide customers. As you review the materials, consider these questions:

1. Are most of these materials easy for the customer to understand?

2. Do the materials provide the customer with telephone numbers to call for additional information?

3. What are your suggestions for improving content?

4. Have you asked customers to review the materials and provide feedback?

5. What additional materials should now be written?

Provide the essential contact information.

Do not end a conversation without providing the customer or referral source with your name and telephone number. Customers must always know how to reach you or your company when the need arises. This is important for several reasons. First, things you think will not go wrong—will. Second, by supplying emergency contact information to your customers, you give them a sense of security, ensuring that you can be easily reached if a problem arises. And the third reason you already know: *People prefer to do business with people who are easy to do business with.* Make sure you and your company fit that description. Customers often save names and telephone numbers in case of a problem. It would be best if the customer called you about the problem rather than spread the word to other referral sources or potential customers. Two things you don't want are (1) customers telling other customers about their inability to reach you, or (2) clients calling case managers or hospital discharge planners complaining about your inaccessibility.

Review Questions

1. Why should you watch your language and tone of voice when talking to customers?

   _____

   _____

   _____

   _____

2. What should you encourage customers to do?

   _____

   _____

   _____

   _____

3. How can you make sure your customer understands?

   _____

   _____

   _____

   _____

4. Why is it important to follow up oral communications with written materials?

   _____

   _____

   _____

   _____

5. Name three reasons why you should always provide contact information.

   _____

   _____

   _____

   _____

7

When Nothing You Do Seems to Work

Objectives

- Recognize the importance of a timely apology.

- Describe ways to continue communication.

- Understand how easy it is to create customer problems.

You have tried many times to make your customer happy. You called him at the hour he requested, sent him duplicate copies of his statements, and explained what his policy covers. You also called family members to re-explain information and contacted doctors at the customer's request. You provided additional copies of reports and even faxed letters instead of mailing them.

Recognize that even with the best intentions, things can go wrong.

For some reason, all that you have done may not be enough. Sometimes things will go wrong no matter how well you or your colleagues handle a situation. Even after you have verified the billing information, checked to see that you have the correct address, or made sure that all the supplies are available for the clinician to make a home visit, problems can arise. With careful monitoring, a corporate quality assurance program, planning and developing a new quality improvement system, problems may still occur.

Be prepared to acknowledge a mistake.

Knowing that problems occur, you need to be prepared to make the first move toward solving them. Some people and systems appear dedicated to creating bumps in the road. You need to be a rock roller dedicated to clearing the path so that customers receive what they need. You also have to have some additional patience left for the next challenge coming your way. Review these suggestions and begin an action plan for your company.

Learn to say you're sorry.

For some customers, a gracious and sincere apology is about all you can offer. Surprisingly, apologizing often proves to be extremely effective in keeping customers happy.

They want it, expect it, and appreciate it. They want it done with sincerity and honesty. They usually have little problem accepting your explanation of how the problem could have happened and are anxious to have it resolved. They, too, want the situation repaired quickly.

When planning to say "I'm sorry," do so with consideration and sincerity. Make the customer feel you care. Just saying you're sorry is not enough. You must consider how it is said and the manner in which it will be received.

Accept that some customers are difficult to please.

You need to accept that for some customers, nothing will work. It may very well be that the anger we attract from customers as health care providers may have nothing to do with what we have said or done. Some customers have been angry at something or someone for most of their lives. We are neither the cause of their problems, nor will we be the solution.

Many patients face great difficulty accepting the limitations caused by their illness. They also may not have the support of their family and friends. Because we are a part of the health care environment, we are seen as obstacles they must endure. For them, there may be little you can do but offer your understanding and support. For this population we may only be able to play a small role in reducing their stress, frustration, or anxiety.

Put your apology in writing.

While some customers may be difficult to work with, a telephone call followed by a sincere letter of apology may be an effective response. You may want to try it since you have nothing to lose and so much to gain. It may very well be worth your time. The letter you send may be shown to their colleagues, family, or friends. This courteous gesture may possibly help convince them your heart and your intentions are in the right place. See Figure 7.1 for a sample letter of apology.

Be willing to go the extra mile.

While you want to avoid having to continually say you're sorry, you can take a risk and ask about what you can do to help them. As you know, this could be a dangerous question and you do need to know your limitations before asking. There can be great satisfaction in addressing exactly what help your customers want and determining if you can meet their needs. Although some customers will be asking for much more than you can provide, the discussion may lead to a workable solution for all parties. You certainly cannot reduce the cost of their insurance, give them free coverage for a specific product, have the home health agency provide free nursing care or free medical equipment, but there may be other services or products you can provide that would keep them happy.

Keep communicating with your customer.

An informed consumer is more likely to remain a customer if he is aware of the reasons the service or product will not be delivered as planned. Keeping in touch is one of the

Figure 7.1   Sample Letter of Apology

A Letter of Apology for a Customer Complaint

Dear _____:

I want to apologize for your having to call our office regarding your recent complaint. I can assure you, your business is extremely important to (name of company) and we want you to be completely satisfied.

It is also important to us that we continue to provide quality service and take the necessary actions to correct any problems we may have caused.

While we are very concerned about your complaint, we are also appreciative of your taking time to call and give us the opportunity to correct the situation. This not only allows us to guarantee your satisfaction 100 percent, but also to prevent the problem from happening to other customers, many of whom would not have taken the extra time to call.

Please accept our sincerest regret for any inconvenience or problems we may have caused you. We took forward to continuing to provide you with the finest service. I hope you will call us at any time with your concerns and allow us to correct any service issue that has not met your expectations.

Thank you for your business. All of us at _____ hope you will accept our apology.

Very truly yours,

William Stevens
Billing Director

best forms of customer service. While you may not be able to prevent a problem, you can at least inform the customer that the problem may occur. Good customer service involves letting people know what they can expect during all stages of the delivery process. If your company has not received the delivery of the wheelchair promised the customer for a particular day, it is important to keep him informed about the delay. Let him know the reason for the delay and what you are doing to correct the situation.

If the nurse is delayed because of a crisis in her family, notify the customer about the situation. If you promised the customer that you were going to mail her some papers via an overnight delivery service and you find that by the end of the day you have not been able to prepare the report, please call to tell her about the delay. While customers may be upset, and apologies do not always work, keeping people informed could reduce some of their anger. Apologize and let them know that you, too, are concerned about being unable to keep your promises.

The more you communicate with your customers, the more apt you are to receive their appreciation. Informed customers are less stressed and anxious and often more understanding.

Help your customer understand all the details.

While we have addressed the value and techniques for good communication, when nothing else seems to work, this often does. Good customer service means helping customers understand the issues related to obtaining authorizations/approval of the billing process for the services you or others may have provided. It means explaining to the patient about the information you need from him and why. Learn to be patient with your customers as you try to help each other. He is unfamiliar with your business, your responsibilities, and methods of operation. You will need to become his health care consultant. The more customers know about a situation or problem, the better able they will be to deal with it and allow you to keep their business.

Maintain your integrity.

As you work at maintaining outstanding customer service levels, you must recognize that everyone makes mistakes. You must come to terms with the fact that even you will some day have to admit your errors and take responsibility for your behavior. It is one of the hardest jobs in the business. When nothing seems to work, simply being honest about your errors will be appreciated. Keep communicating. People prefer to do business with people who offer an honest and open relationship. While you may not be able to get everything right, the customer will admire your values.

Review Questions

1. What's your best option when you can't make the customer happy?

   _____

   _____

   _____

   _____

2. Why would a customer project anger at you when you did nothing to deserve it?

   _____

   _____

   _____

   _____

3. Why is it important to keep communicating?

   _____

   _____

   _____

   _____

4. What's the best way to handle your error?

   _____

   _____

   _____

   _____

8

Telephone Strategies

Objectives

- Develop protocols for handling customer calls.
- Learn tips for using phone mail and taking messages.

With the telephone being the front line in most health care businesses, it is an office tool that needs special attention. A telephone sits on almost every desk in your office. Many offices are also equipped with a phone mail system to intercept calls when you are not at your desk. However, if you're sitting right next to the phone when it rings, pick it up. It's a bad business practice not to answer customer calls, yet you may be surprised how often calls go unanswered. Maybe you've heard some of these excuses.

"I would answer it but I don't know what to say."

Learn what to say when you pick up the telephone. The greeting should be: Good morning (good afternoon), _____ (company name), this is _____ (your name). How may I help you?

(Example: Good morning, Alpha Health Advisors. This is Louis. How may I help you?)

Customers want verification that they have called the correct business or office. They also want to know the name of the person with whom they are speaking.

"I do not know how to transfer a call."

Learn the mechanics of transferring calls to the appropriate person. Ask the people who sold you the telephone system to provide you with the necessary training. All new staff members should have telephone training as part of their orientation program. If that is not being done, take out the manual, make copies of the instructions to hand out to employees, and make sure every employee knows how to transfer a call.

"I do not know how to locate other people in the company."

Place a company directory next to each phone. If your directory is on line, make sure every employee knows how to access it. The directory should list everyone working in the organization, including telephone numbers, titles, and departments. You want to refer the customer to the right person the first time. You do not want a call coming back to you because it was forwarded to the wrong department. Both your customers and fellow colleagues will find this annoying. Staff members may unknowingly express their frustration to the customer when they receive a call that was not intended for them. Have you ever overheard or been asked, "Why did they refer your call to me?" You don't want to waste the customer's time by misrouting a call.

As you develop your company telephone directory, include other important information about your organization, such as work hours, services menu, product list, as well as numbers to call in an emergency.

Your Company Directory

What would you include in your company directory?

1. _____

2. _____

3. _____

4. _____

5. _____

"I am afraid they will ask something I know nothing about."

Information about the company—what it offers and how it functions—should be included in all employee orientation programs. With the introduction or termination of a new program or service, it is important to make sure every employee is notified. Every employee must know as much as possible about the organization and its products.

The answers to frequently asked questions should be provided in corporate training. If this didn't happen, and you and fellow employees are not getting the information you need, you may have to champion the cause. Ask your marketing department to prepare **product fact sheets,** one-page documents that list key product features, describe benefits, identify target market, and provide price and ordering information. Put the issue of training on the front burner at staff meetings. It's in your organization's best interests to supply the training to keep the staff knowledgeable.

Let's face it, there may be times when you can't answer a customer's question immediately. When this happens, you need to be committed to doing the research, finding the answer, and getting back to the customer quickly. Those first few seconds when the customer makes contact with your office can be vital to her future decision as to whether she will ever call your company again.

Think about when you've made business calls. Do you have a horror story to tell? How about being put on hold forever; listening to a series of recorded messages with no way of connecting to a live person; pressing zero for the operator and being disconnected. These are commonplace experiences. The point is that you don't want your company taking a leading role in the horror stories. Pay attention to how calls are handled. Pretend you're a customer and call your company. Find out about the glitches so you can fix them. Here are some protocols to consider when reviewing how your company uses the telephone.

Monitor your system to determine if you are losing calls.

Are there more calls coming in than you are able to answer? Have your telephone company assist you in monitoring your lost calls. If you are unable to handle the large volume of calls you receive, management may have to make some staffing or system changes. Lost calls cost your company business. Customers will assume you are too busy to pick up the telephone.

Answer with the same greeting and energy throughout the day.

Use the same greeting no matter what time of the day the call is received. While you may be leaving your office when the phone rings, to the customer you must appear happy to receive their call. The customer expects the same service and greeting no matter when the call is placed. Be consistent in your telephone greeting.

Use reminders for voice mail.

Many people who have a voice mail system forget to review their messages. If needed, place a reminder on your phone to check your messages. People have been known to leave messages on voice mail for days. Your business cannot afford to neglect important messages.

Learn how to take a message.

Taking telephone messages may seem like a no-brainer, yet all too often the person taking the message is not careful about getting detailed information. All messages should note time, date, and signature of the person taking the call. The signature on the message helps you locate the person who took the call so you can further clarify information. Many messages contain transposed numbers, misspelled names, and the like. Be careful to get the correct information. Your attention to detail will save a lot of time.

Decide where to place the messages.

If you are taking messages for someone else, agree upon a place where you will leave all of her messages. Do not change the plan unless you verify with the person you are working with. You do not want to misplace or lose any messages.

Your Telephone Test

Think about your last call and then decide if you:

	Yes	No
Answered the telephone in three rings.	_____	_____
Answered with energy and enthusiasm.	_____	_____
Clearly identified your name and the company name.	_____	_____
Had paper and pencil handy to take notes/messages.	_____	_____
Showed interest in the caller.	_____	_____
Asked questions for clarity.	_____	_____
Promised specific actions.	_____	_____

Taking a Message

Review the last message you took and see if you got everything right:

• Caller's name (correct spelling)	_____ Yes	_____ No
• Caller's organization	_____ Yes	_____ No
• Caller's complete telephone number	_____ Yes	_____ No
• Caller's message	_____ Yes	_____ No
• Date and time of call	_____ Yes	_____ No
• Name of person who took the message	_____ Yes	_____ No
• Confirmed the details of any promises	_____ Yes	_____ No
• Thanked the caller for calling	_____ Yes	_____ No

Concentrate on what the caller is saying.

Your attitude on the telephone is extremely important for obtaining the information that you need to assist the customer. Provide undivided attention to the customer throughout the conversation. You want to avoid having to call the customer back to clarify information.

Handling the telephone has become an art form. To be effective and efficient you will need training, experience, and reminders. Every time the telephone rings, watch your attitude. Stay focused on what you need to do to handle the call effectively and how you can rapidly access the information that your customer needs. Just wait a moment and you can practice on the call coming in.

Review Questions

1. What are some excuses people use for not answering the telephone at work?

   _____
   _____
   _____
   _____

2. Why are the excuses unacceptable?

   _____
   _____
   _____
   _____

3. What are pertinent details a message taker needs to note?

   _____
   _____
   _____
   _____

4. What are some protocols for handling customer calls?

   _____
   _____
   _____
   _____

5. Why should you give the caller your undivided attention?

   _____
   _____
   _____
   _____

9

How to Learn About Your Customer

Objectives

- Develop strategies for gathering information.
- Understand the value of an organizational chart.
- Identify customer survey methods.

Getting to know more about your customer is one of the best ways to improve service. To be successful, a business must fully understand its customers' needs and the venue in which services are provided. In the health care environment, the rules of the game are never static because of constantly changing reimbursement requirements. Legislative issues affect all of us—professional and consumer—and one needs to be involved in the industry on a daily basis to keep up. As industry insiders, we are challenged by information overload. We must monitor new developments in health affairs, technology, and clinical practice, as well as interpret and clarify information about new advances, so that we can advise our clients and consumers.

There is much to learn about what is happening outside your business that could affect your customers. For starters, you need to know what your customers are thinking and experiencing. At least 10 percent of your time should be devoted to learning about your customers. Which products and services do they want? How and when do they need your service? What makes each of your customers unique? No two customers are the same. For example, each professional customer has his or her own way of doing business. A case manager, social worker, or insurance agent may have different preferences for how they want to receive communications. Are you aware of the differences? Do you know who wants you to e-mail information and who prefers a telephone call?

There are many ways to track and gather information about your customers. You can use a software program for developing a database or use traditional paper and pencil. The following suggestions will help you understand different approaches.

1. Develop an account assessment system.

Begin documenting customer service information that you obtain. Keep a dedicated record for each account. This information can be placed in a file or in a specific software program used for managing accounts. Review and update your customer records monthly.

2. If appropriate, document the organizational structure of the company/customer you are working with.

Ask for an **organization chart** or attempt to develop your own if your contact is unable to share one with you. An organization chart lets you see how a system is structured, by graphically depicting various departments, roles or functions, and hierarchy. Learn the names of the company managers, departments they manage, and how they can be reached. Learn who reports to whom. The more you understand about the operation of the organizations that you work with, the better able you will be to meet their needs.

Schedule meetings with key customers to learn about their customer service needs and to determine if what you offer meets their expectations or if you will have to change some of your operations to keep them satisfied. Are you working with key decision makers as noted on the organization chart?

3. Create a customer needs assessment.

Begin by identifying why your customer is calling your company. What is it that attracted them to your business? Did someone refer them? Is there someone you need to thank for the referral? Referral sources are also customers.

Your **needs assessment** of the customer should begin during the initial contact. Gather as much data about the customer as possible. This is information customers usually tire of repeating but you need to hear. Make sure you have all the correct contact information. Check the spelling of names and get a clear description of special needs or requests. Your ability to access basic information about the customer quickly will impress her later on.

In your account record, document any information you have provided the customer and materials they have requested. You need to identify all materials that have already been sent and what additional reports or documents may be of value. All of this information should be placed in one folder or computer file for easy access.

4. Develop written customer service surveys.

We discuss the importance of customer surveys in other chapters. Record information obtained in surveys in the customer assessment file. In the survey questionnaire, you'll want to have customers evaluate the services you offer and report on their direct experiences with particular company departments. When you send out your survey package, make sure that you enclose a self-addressed, stamped envelope. You must do everything possible to make it convenient for the recipient to complete and return the survey form. Set up a schedule; and if the survey isn't returned by a target date, call the customer to remind them about how much you value their opinion and to please complete and return the survey to your office.

5. Conduct telephone interviews with your customers.

Telephone interviews can work if you follow certain guidelines. Realize that even if you ask all the right questions you may not get the whole story. First, consider the person you have selected to conduct the interview. Often it is best to employ someone outside of your organization to handle the calls. You'll need to develop a script so your interviewer will know exactly what to ask. The person calling the customer should tell the client that she is not with the company being evaluated. This is not only the best approach, but having a neutral party make the calls will enable your customer to provide a more honest and open response.

You may want to mail an introductory letter a week or so prior to the telephone survey, notifying the customer that he will be contacted soon. Let him know that an outside firm employed by the organization he has done business with will be calling to speak with him. The customer may want to prepare his thoughts or arrange for the appropriate person to take the call.

Be aware of the time of day you are calling. Try to avoid calling professionals at work during the first hour in the morning, during meal times, or at the close of the day. Mid-morning and mid-afternoon are the best times. If they are at home during the day, patients and consumers may be accepting of calls at other hours, depending on their schedules. Always be flexible and willing to call the consumer back at a more convenient time.

Be careful in selecting the person who will conduct the interviews for your organization. Her personality, the sound of her voice, and her attitude are important factors for successfully obtaining honest and meaningful information. You should look for someone with a pleasant voice, nonthreatening approach, and a comprehensive understanding of your business. If you're hiring an outside firm to conduct the interviews, you may want to monitor calls to check the interviewer's performance.

Recommendations for Surveyor

Identify three people in your company you feel could conduct a telephone interview and solicit an honest and open response from the customer.

1. _____

2. _____

3. _____

If you are calling professional customers or referral sources, avoid calling on Mondays. People are extra busy on Mondays handling messages and solving problems that happened over the weekend. Wednesdays and Thursdays are known to be less pressured days for most health care professionals. If time permits, maybe your customer would be willing to complete the survey over lunch or coffee. This may be a more relaxed time with few office or business distractions.

Remember, when you are completing the survey, you are taking people away from their work to help you improve your company. While some may welcome the diversion, others may see it as a distraction. Allot as much time as you can. For you, this is an important part of getting educated about the customer.

Make sure you begin the conversation by thanking the customer for their time. Verify that you are speaking with someone who can provide you the information you are seeking and that you are calling at a convenient time. If this is not a good time, ask when it would be better for them to have you call back. Never ask the customer to call you back. It's your survey, not theirs.

6. Schedule face-to-face interviews with your customers.

While **face-to-face meetings** are difficult to arrange, they are the most interesting and valuable way to solicit information. You can see the expressions on the faces of your customers and make eye contact. What issues are they eager to talk about? What topics seem to be avoided? Are there topics they are willing to talk about in person but probably would not have mentioned in a written survey? Since many customers are reluctant to call you with their problems (sometimes hard to believe), face-to-face meetings may be the only time you will hear about what is important to them.

7. Complete annual customer reports.

Your customers need to know more about you. While you may not be creating a year-end company report, it may be valuable to supply one for your customers. An update about your operation is a promotional tool, and lets the customer learn more about you, as you continue to learn about her. Publicly held stock companies send out annual reports and so should you. Think of it as an opportunity to market your services and showcase your successes.

Your **annual customer report** can come in the form of a newsletter or brochure outlining new services, introducing staff, or describing programs and issues that would be important to the customer. You may want to report any changes in the organization that would affect the services he receives. Announce improvements that will make it easier and more efficient to work with your organization. Your annual report is a key part of your customer retention program, giving you yet another opportunity to thank your customer for their business.

Getting to know the customer is not something that will happen automatically. It takes planning—an organized approach. Not matter what method you choose—do something. You cannot effectively serve a customer whom you do not understand. You cannot develop programs and services that will sell unless you know that they are wanted and ultimately will be purchased. Customers are your very best source for training. They will provide you more information than you ever expected.

Review Questions

1. Why is it important to get to know each customer?

   _____

   _____

   _____

   _____

2. What is an effective tool for archiving customer data?

   _____

   _____

   _____

   _____

3. How can an organization chart assist you?

   _____

   _____

   _____

   _____

4. Describe three methods for obtaining information from the customer.

   _____

   _____

   _____

   _____

5. What traits should you look for in a telephone interviewer?

   _____

   _____

   _____

   _____

PART THREE

Improving Customer Service

10

How to Verify the Quality of Your Services

Objectives

- Describe the value of direct contact with your customers.

- Understand how customers can help you improve your service.

- Identify strategies for verifying your service.

You may think you have been providing the best customer service, so you may be surprised to learn what your customers really think. Often our egos prevent us from forming an objective picture of our business operation.

One of the most effective methods for keeping in touch with reality is by maintaining contact with your customers. They are your best consultants. The better the relationship you have with the customers, the greater the probability that you will learn from them. They can tell you what they like and do not like about your company. Find out what would cause them to go to a different provider. Is it the way you send them information, provide follow-up data, or refer them to so many other people just to have simple questions answered? The more you talk to customers and listen to their comments, the more you will learn about your business. The following suggestions will help you verify the quality of your services.

1. Verify that you have given correct information about products or services.

If you were not the one to deliver the product or service, this will be an even more important call. Your goal is to correct any misinformation or customer problems. You want to verify that what the customer expected was provided. By making sure the customer receives what she needs, you will reduce the number of problems that can occur if you do it "wrong" the first time. It will also help your customer become an informed consumer.

2. Call your customers within 24 hours of the delivery of a service or product.

This important call can help stem the flow of negative comments in case the delivery did not go as planned. Have the customer tell you what happened to him when dealing with your company. What does he think about the person who delivered the service? How would he describe the attitude and demeanor of the service provider? It is better for you to learn about a customer's concern or problem before he shares the story with other professionals or potential customers.

3. Verify that you have sent the information or products requested.

When customers do not receive what they expect, they can become angry. They may have received a product and now realize it is the wrong one. The report they received may have been missing important information, or the policy you spoke about was not the one mailed. If what they received is not correct, you can control the damage and correct the problem before they start contacting their network of professionals or friends. Take time to verify that all expectations were met and that what was agreed upon was delivered.

4. Provide each customer with a customer service survey.

Prepare the survey so that it can be quickly completed and easily mailed back to your company. A written survey allows each customer to express how she feels about the service and to do it without having to tell you in person. The mail-in survey may provide a more comfortable vehicle for a customer to express her real feelings. You, too, may find the responses easier to digest, especially the negative comments.

There are, however, those who have difficulty writing about how they feel and will provide a more accurate response if you speak with them personally. They may be reluctant to write their comments. By calling patients, families, or business colleagues, you can get first-person accounts of a situation, and gain more information than you would ever learn through a written report.

Remember to thank everyone you speak with for taking time to share their thoughts. Tell them their contribution is important for improving the services you provide to all of your customers. Send a brief thank-you note to follow up on your telephone interview.

Your survey results will be more valuable if you analyze your responses from pre-selected groups of customers. The demographics you should consider are:

- customer's location,

- work location for professional customers/referral sources,

- jobs of professional customer/referral sources, and

- types of services requested.

Look at the sample script included as Figure 10.1 for tips on preparing your customer service survey.

Figure 10.1   Sample Customer Service Survey Script

Customer Service Survey

Hello, my name is _____ .

I am with _____(organization)_____ and in our effort to provide outstanding customer service, I would be very appreciative if you could answer a few short questions about your feelings concerning the services we provided on _____(date)_____ .

1. How did you hear about our company? _____
2. Were you pleased with the service we provided? ____ Yes   ____ No
3. If not, why not? _____
4. Did we meet your expectations? ____ Yes   ____ No
5. If not, what did you expect that was not received or done? _____
6. Would you call us again if you needed the same service? ____ Yes   ____ No
7. Would you refer our company to someone else in need of the same service? ____ Yes   ____ No
8. Do you have any recommendations for improving our services? _____
9. What did you like least about how we worked with you? _____
10. What did you like most about us? _____

For a business referral account, ask these additional questions:
1. Have we helped make your work responsibilities easier to handle? ____ Yes   ____ No
2. If not, why not? _____
3. If yes, how? _____
4. Are you aware of any comments by your customers regarding the services we provided?
5. Are we presently not providing you any information or products that we should? _____
6. Can our company be of any further assistance to you? ____ Yes   ____ No
7. If yes, how? _____

Ask the customer to rate your service. Here are some examples:
1. How satisfied are you with _____?
   ____ Very satisfied   ____ Satisfied   ____ Neutral   ____ Dissatisfied   ____ Very dissatisfied.
2. Please rate our customer service.
   ____ Excellent   ____ Good   ____ Average   ____ Fair   ____ Poor
3. Our company provides great customer service.
   ____ Strongly agree   ____ Agree   ____ Neutral   ____ Disagree   ____ Strongly disagree
4. How often does our customer service exceed expectations?
   ____ Very frequently   ____ Frequently   ____ Not sure   ____ Infrequently
   ____ Very infrequently

Some additional characteristics to rate:
❑ Ethical behavior
❑ Listening to customers
❑ Phone calls answered quickly
❑ Politeness of those answering the telephone
❑ Continually placing customers on hold
❑ Avoiding customer complaints

❑ Ability to reach specific people
❑ Attention to details
❑ Friendliness
❑ Staff interested in helping you
❑ Knowledgeable staff

5. Ask for recommendations for improving your service.

When surveying customers, find out what makes them happy. Ask for suggestions for improving the communication process. Determine which method of communication is preferred (for example, personal meetings and face-to-face interactions, e-mail, telephone, fax, or letter). Whatever method is selected and agreed upon, use it as a means for further communication.

Other methods for gathering information include focus groups and face-to-face interviews. Customers may contribute interesting ideas for you to consider as you design new forms, develop patient education programs, and seek ways to improve delivery schedules, information systems, or your in-bound telephone center. Ask and you will receive.

6. Evaluate the service delivered by your competitors.

You need to call your competitors, visit their stores, and learn from your customers about their experiences with other providers. What special systems, products, or services are keeping your competitors in business? What has impressed customers and you about your competitors? Can lessons be learned from observing the way they do business? They have been able to retain customers for years and it would be important for you to understand the ingredients of their success. By comparing yourself to the competition, you can identify your strengths and weaknesses. When was the last time you called a rival business to see how quickly they pick up their telephone? Did they efficiently handle your questions?

Develop a list of what your customers prefer about your competition and what they like about you. It will provide some interesting reading and talking points for your next staff meeting.

Evaluating Your Competitors

What customer service behaviors give your competitors business advantages?

List four behaviors that you would like to incorporate into your organization.

1. _____

2. _____

3. _____

4. _____

What would it take to make these changes in your operation?

_____

Review
Questions

1. How can you verify that your customer has received accurate information about a product or service?

_____

_____

_____

_____

2. When and why should you call the customer after a product or service has been delivered?

_____

_____

_____

_____

3. What methods can you use to survey customers?

_____

_____

_____

_____

4. Why is it important to obtain information about your competitors?

_____

_____

_____

_____

11

How to Analyze the Service Cycles of Your Business

Objectives

- Review how each department interacts with the customer.

- Identify potential service blocks.

- Create a flowchart depicting the service cycle.

Every department or section in your company works both as a specialized team and in conjunction with other units. Your company may have its own customer service department with a team working together to provide service to the buyers of your products. To ensure a smooth flow in the service continuum, it is wise to examine the processes. Look at how the customer connects with each department. Evaluate how well each unit interacts with the customer and coordinates services down the line. Does the clinical team talk to the billing department? Does marketing have promotional materials reviewed by customer service representatives or potential customers? Do delivery technicians understand what the customer intake department does?

In every company **service units**—departments, work groups, or individuals—provide certain functions or activities to fulfill customer requests. Each unit represents a step in a process by which a service or product is delivered.

The customer enters your organization from some defined and selected point, such as an initial telephone call. They may have obtained your telephone number from the telephone book, an advertisement, or a brochure that they received in the mail. Maybe they noticed a sign on the door and simply walked into your office. Perhaps the initial call was precipitated because a friend or physician suggested your name. The reason should always be documented as it can affect the foundation of the relationship. For example, if a customer is referred by another happy customer, you could expect a more positive relationship right from the beginning. You want the relationship to go well, so start off with a warm and welcome greeting.

To understand how the system can operate with minimum problems, you should develop a chart or graph depicting the service cycle and identifying all the stages that a customer/call/order travels through to reach the delivery point. What you are developing is a map or **flowchart** outlining the customer's path from the first time they contact you to the time they receive the product they are requesting. Even if the customer is calling for a third or fourth time, each call and interaction is routed and handled in some particular way. For example, to reach the doctor the patient may need to speak with two people since the person receiving the call may not take messages. For the case manager to order oxygen for a patient, she may first speak with a respiratory therapist. Take a moment and think about how those initial calls and requests are handled in your office.

Some of the stages or events may include: (1) picking up the telephone in a timely manner, (2) obtaining customer contact information, (3) preparing a document/proposal for the customer, (4) preparing a bill for processing, (5) auditing the final product before delivery, and (6) actually delivering the product to the customer. There are many steps in the **customer service cycle**. Just think about all the steps that are taken once the physician calls the hospital to order special medication for a patient. What happens once the order is received? How many people may get involved besides the person taking the order? A nurse, pharmacist, technician—who else?

Begin thinking of all the points of contact the customer reaches before he is in actual receipt of what he wants. At each stage there will be requirements for particular behaviors you or the customer may need to follow. These may need to be accomplished before the patient or customer can progress to the next stage and ultimately receive what he requested.

Because the receptionist in your office is able to pick up the telephone in two or three rings, what happens then? Is everyone in the office as responsive to the telephone ringing? When a customer calls your office about information regarding an insurance claim, does she talk to one or two people before she reaches the person with the answers? The more people she speaks with, the greater the likelihood that problems will occur.

The following example of how a medical equipment order was taken will help you understand what can go wrong.

A call from the discharge planner at Seashore Hospital comes into the office. The person answering the telephone places the caller on hold only to lose the call. The discharge planner calls back. The order is finally taken but the address is not complete. The delivery technician receives the order but sees no reason to verify the address, although the street is unfamiliar to him. He does not have a map in the van. He spends an hour making what should have been a 15-minute delivery. When he arrives at the patient's home, he knows the patient must complete and sign necessary forms, but since he was running late he has forgotten to bring them with him from the office or to see if he has additional forms in the van. He returns to the office with incomplete paperwork. The billing department does not realize this until several days after the product is delivered.

Do you get the picture? Are you starting to see where one supposedly simple order and delivery can become a nightmare?

It is time to recognize and define all the challenges customers can face and to learn the importance of understanding each segment of the service cycle. For each step, you need to list all the activities that should and could take place. For example, in the first stage of the customer contact, the telephone rings and someone should answer it in three rings. The person answering the telephone can handle the caller, take a message, or transfer the call to the appropriate person.

What could happen? The telephone is not answered in a timely manner, or the person answering is not sure where to locate the telephone number of the person the caller is asking for, or there is no pencil or paper near the telephone to take a message. The list of possible problems goes on.

You need to continue to look at all the steps in the service cycle and list what could go wrong at each point. Think about how you can avoid misinterpreting information, obtaining wrong telephone numbers, or providing the delivery staff with incomplete instructions. Come up with solutions—like having delivery technicians carry maps.

Checklists may help you through this process. Make a list of activities that must be done in each stage of the service cycle. This will ensure that you do all that you need to do when you need to do it. Your goal is to avoid problems before they happen. By reviewing all aspects of the service cycle, you will learn to pinpoint what could go wrong, and then set up a plan for doing things right the first time—all the time.

Take a careful look at your own organization and make a flowchart of the operation. The exercise that follows will help you analyze your department, business, or operation.

Creating a Service Cycle for Your Business

Where do calls travel within your organization and what problems occur during each of these stops?

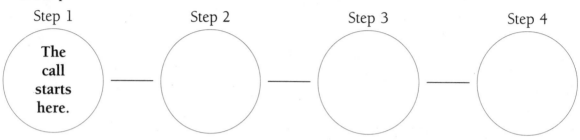

Step 1   Step 2   Step 3   Step 4

The call starts here.

Step 1: What can go wrong during this first attempt to communicate with your company? What problems can happen as the telephone rings?

1. _____

2. _____

Step 2: What can go wrong when the call is transferred to the next department?

1. _____

2. _____

Step 3: Who would be the next person the customer deals with and what could go wrong during this next interaction/stage?

1. _____

2. _____

Step 4: How do you end the interaction with the customer?

1. _____

2. _____

Evaluate all the stages that customers must go through before finally receiving the service, product, or answer they are requesting.

Review Questions

1. What is a service cycle?

_____
_____
_____
_____

2. What tool can you use to show how a customer/call/order travels through your organization?

_____
_____
_____
_____

3. What should you look for when mapping out your service system?

_____
_____
_____
_____

4. Why should you examine all aspects of your operation?

_____
_____
_____
_____

5. How can a checklist help you avoid problems?

_____
_____
_____
_____

12

Criteria for Evaluating the Quality of Service

Objectives

- Identify criteria that customers use to evaluate a company.

- Define criteria for service analysis.

- Increase awareness of competency problems.

Many elements in your daily business life can affect the way customers perceive the quality of your services. Families, patients, and professional referral sources have their own unique set of standards. Each individual reviews your work from his or her own perspective. Customers look for certain signs of efficiency, caring, and dedication to determine if you care about them and their business.

Since your entire health care operation can be placed under a microscope, you must conduct your own evaluations of your department or organization. We must see for ourselves where we can improve our customer services before our faults become apparent to the customer. In the following sections you'll find a list of characteristics you should examine—tangible and intangible items that can reveal a lot about an organization. Take a look at these magical seven components, cast a critical eye at your operation, discuss your critique with your colleagues, and then determine how you would rate your company.

Appearance

Evaluate the appearance of your business, your products, and your colleagues. Customers who come into your office or facility often judge you by what they see. This is the reason many companies have their staff wear uniforms. Do you need to clear away some of those old boxes sitting on your floor? Have you taken down those messages posted on the bulletin board last year? Should you clean up your desk and discard the mail you opened weeks ago and have yet to handle?

What the customer sees first often sets the tone of the relationship. In other words, your customer's observations may influence her expectations. She may start to question whether she can trust your promises or your real willingness to help. Perhaps she will notice the chaos or sense the calmness in your office. How do you think she would rate your office environment?

Reliability

Do you keep your promises? Do you deliver what your customer is expecting? Can your office be trusted to do what you say you are going to do? You need to determine if your customers see you as a reliable organization. Make note of customers who call you once or only seek services once. Contacting and interviewing customers who have not returned may provide you with interesting data about how reliable others think you are. Many professionals need to sense the reliability of their colleagues, too.

Responsiveness

Is your service prompt and efficient? Do you apologize for keeping people waiting? Do you maintain your schedule of meetings or appointments? Do you recognize the true value of the customer's requests, comments, and suggestions? Being responsive means being customer-focused. Realize that every interaction with the customer is an opportunity for proving your ability to meet his needs in a timely manner.

Communication

Do you carefully explain your services and products, reimbursement issues, and treatment plans in customer-friendly language so that customers/referral sources fully understand? If requested, do you willingly and graciously explain issues more than once? Patients are often nervous and upset and may need several explanations of unfamiliar information. Do you encourage questions? Make the effort to speak in a language the customer understands and never be annoyed at having to explain anything more than once.

Any communication with the customer—by letter, newsletter, call, etc.—lets her know you are thinking about her. You may want to let her know that you have additional materials or information to help her. Timely communication can be a factor in reducing the customer's stress.

Competence

Do you and your associates have the necessary knowledge to assist your customers effectively and appropriately? Are you continually updating your skills? Review the list of in-service programs scheduled for your department during the next several months. Is there a list? Make your manager or supervisor aware of your educational needs. Begin creating a series of programs for building your competency. Knowledge is a powerful tool in improving customer service. For example, if there is a new reimbursement program or service available, make sure each employee who interacts with the customer understands the new program and can explain its features and benefits. Customers will appreciate your ability to handle the complex customer service questions.

In-Service Educational Needs

Identify four subject areas that you would like addressed in future in-service training programs:

1. _____
2. _____
3. _____
4. _____

Where can you locate information or speakers who can provide you with the information you need?

_____

Courtesy

Are you always polite, saying "please" and "thank you" when appropriate? Do you show respect for the customer, maintain a friendly attitude, and exhibit empathy for their problems and issues? Do you treat nurses or case managers who call you with the same courtesy and respect with which you treat the end-user of your products/services? Showing common courtesy, the kind learned in childhood, is one of the best customer service strategies, and its practice can lay the foundation for profitable, long-term business relationships. How about your company?

Understanding

Do you make an effort to know and understand the needs of your customer and how you can meet those needs? When the patient or social worker is talking, are you listening? Are you asking the right types of questions to gather sufficient information about the customer so that you can be helpful and effective in meeting his needs? Getting feedback from the customer is a critical component of knowing what your customer wants and detecting if you are meeting his expectations consistently.

Rating Your Health Care Company

How do you rate your company?	Out-standing	Very Good	Good	Fair	Poor
Tangible Appearance	1	2	3	4	5
Reliability	1	2	3	4	5
Responsiveness	1	2	3	4	5
Communication	1	2	3	4	5
Competency	1	2	3	4	5
Courtesy	1	2	3	4	5
Knowing/Understanding the Customer	1	2	3	4	5

Review Questions

1. What are some of the qualities that customers look for in a service provider?

   _____

   _____

   _____

   _____

2. Why should you be proactive in conducting an evaluation of your department or organization?

   _____

   _____

   _____

   _____

3. Why is it important to pay attention to the physical appearance of your office?

   _____

   _____

   _____

   _____

4. What are some of the other characteristics of service that you should examine?

   _____

   _____

   _____

   _____

13

How to Monitor Four Key Problem Areas

Objectives

- Understand the value of checklists for monitoring service.

- Identify four key problem areas.

- Understand why it is important to distribute lots of information.

Many companies are on a never-ending quest for effective monitoring techniques. It is important to catch problems before they negatively affect the operation. The most difficult task is deciding what you want to monitor and where to begin. For many people, taking the first step can be the most difficult.

Following is a short list of potential problems areas. Once you begin examining the service cycles of your business, you will uncover many more issues of concern. These four are the easiest to identify and should be the first places you look for potential problems.

Monitor #1—On-time delivery

Many of your customers could be waiting for you to call them back, mail them insurance information, or provide them a clearer explanation of something they do not understand. Some customers may be waiting at home for a clinician or caregiver to arrive. They were given a time when they could expect the service, a call, or a product to be delivered; and now they are waiting to see if what was promised will be delivered on time.

Homebound patients expecting a nurse to visit or a product to be delivered at a particular time often begin waiting during the early hours of the day hoping for an earlier than expected arrival. Your home care customer may spend many hours waiting for you, even though you told him that you would not be there until after three in the afternoon.

To ensure a positive relationship with the customer from the start, make sure you arrive on time—or even a little before your scheduled appointment. You want to pass this first test the customer could be giving you and your organization. It is important to meet this initial customer expectation. In an effort to determine what causes late deliveries and how they can be avoided, you must monitor what is happening.

Monitor incoming calls and determine if the telephone is being answered by the third ring. Is your mail arriving at your customer's office as you promised? How quickly is the person you asked to fax the report to the physician's office actually doing it? Are people responding to customer requests according to company standards? If there are no standards or protocols, it is time to write them.

Monitor #2—Tracking and reporting

Keep the customer informed about any delays that may occur in the process of delivering the service or product to his home or office. Who is responsible for calling the customer to notify him of a potential problem? If someone is waiting for a product or a piece of mail to be delivered, can you locate any of the shipping documentation to see what may be causing the delay? How does your organization handle these issues?

How will the customer be informed if you have finally received the product that you in turn will be delivering to her? How will the customer be notified to pick up the product if that is the agreement? Ongoing communication prevents tension, often created when the customer feels neglected, or even worse—forgotten. What is scary is that she may have actually been forgotten.

Monitor #3—Handling problems and complaints

Think about what happens after the product or service is delivered. In a comprehensive quality management and improvement program, follow-up service is an important part of the process. First, systems must be in place for checking reports, materials, and products before they are delivered to the customer. If you are a nurse delivering supplies to a patient's home, you should create a checklist to identify what you need to bring with you. If you are a medical equipment technician delivering an electric bed, you will need to include the correct patient instruction materials, documents requiring the customer's signature, and business cards for any patient follow-up.

Many business relationships are only put to the real test after the first documents or products are delivered. Developing checklists will help you monitor your activities, defining what needs to be done prior to, during, and after the service and/or delivery has been completed. Make sure you are bringing to the customer all that is promised. It not only angers the customer when he does not receive what he expected, but he can become infuriated when he cannot locate anyone to assist him once he has already paid for the service. Your commitment to the customer after you have received his money will help him understand the value you have placed on his business. Develop a system, select a person, and create a program for keeping in touch with your customers. Someone has to do it and it might as well be you.

Monitor #4—Providing information

Beyond the standard literature you provide customers describing products they purchased, you may need to supply additional information. Unfortunately, professional writers and technicians, who may have had little customer contact, are often the authors of patient or product instruction materials. Always check the literature that goes to your customer and make sure that the instructions are reader friendly.

Home care nurses may need to bring additional copies of patient instruction manuals to share with other family members. Interview your customer to determine what she does or does not understand. Consider rewriting customer or patient instructions, using terminology that is easy to understand, and adding graphics or colors to make the piece eye-catching. Remember to distribute product information to your business colleagues who need to stay abreast of new developments in your industry.

You do not want the customer to purchase a product or service that he does not fully understand. Before you leave your office for an appointment, create a checklist of items to bring with you. Make sure you carry a supply of printed handouts highlighting the important issues to be discussed with the client. The patient may need to repeat what you have said to someone else. The insurance agent may need to make a presentation to a group unfamiliar with insurance terminology. The literature you provide can be used as a resource. Make yourself a reminder to bring additional copies of customer-oriented information just in case more people show up at your meeting than you originally expected.

Be aware of what customers are saying about the materials you share with them. Are they asking for additional information? Is the information focused on the needs of a particular audience? The written marketing materials developed for a beneficiary/consumer may not be the same as those needed by a case manager, social worker, or hospital insurance department. Monitor what you are distributing, always checking with your clients to see if the information is helpful.

Review Questions

1. Why is it important to show up early for a first appointment with a client?

_____

_____

_____

_____

2. Why should you always maintain a delivery tracking system?

_____

_____

_____

_____

3. How would a checklist help you?

_____

_____

_____

_____

4. What would a client do with additional copies of your literature or product manual?

_____

_____

_____

_____

PART FOUR

Managing, Staffing, and Training

14

How to Manage Your Customer Service Operation

Objectives

- Identify leadership qualities of the person in charge.

- Review selection criteria for the customer service committee.

- Define how standards should be developed and instituted.

Throughout the text we have discussed strategies for improving customer service and creating a customer-driven organization. While the concepts guiding excellent service are not difficult to understand, the real challenge comes when we begin to develop standards and initiate quality improvement programs.

As new companies enter the marketplace, they try to learn from established businesses. Your competition wants to know how you built your business and what you do to sustain profits. They also want to know about your weaknesses: Is the quality of your customer service consistent? How can they capitalize on your mistakes? While you are spending time correcting problems, your competitors may be building new relationships by talking to customers who have become frustrated with the way you do business.

Competition should drive you to action. Every organization needs a dedicated customer service program, supported and managed by key employees. The following sections provide a 10-step guide to help you launch a program at your location.

1. Assess the need.

Your survival is at stake. The customer wants the best service. Competition continues to improve, and there are more companies entering the market. You need to know how well your operation is doing if you want to meet or exceed the customer's expectations. If you do not take care of the customer, many other companies are willing to fill the void.

2. Appoint a program director.

To move forward, you must do more than talk about your service problems. It is time to find someone to lead the cause. Select a person everyone respects and admires; someone who can model behavior for others to follow. This person does not need to be a supervisor or manager, but should be someone with the following attributes:

- relates well to people at all levels of the organization;

- has the ability to schedule and authorize training programs;

- has budget responsibility and can obtain money for training;

- understands accountability;

- has the respect of the entire organization;

- will take the program seriously;

- can communicate effectively with supervisors and a board of directors if one exists;

- has a vision for the entire operation; and

- has experience interacting with patients, providers, and other segments of the industry.

It must be someone with a broad organizational perspective, who understands how each department interrelates with the next and how important it is for all employees to be involved in customer service training. Look for a person who has patience and understanding. The appointment of a program director will change your corporate culture, initiating new ways of thinking about all customer interactions. You want to put a true leader in charge.

3. Form a customer service committee.

Before selecting members for this committee think about its mission and make sure everyone who participates in developing standards and programs understands the focus is on meeting customers' needs. Find out which people have an interest in serving on such a committee. The person who spearheads the search project need not be the chair of the committee. Try to include staff members from various departments. You will get very different perspectives on customer service from each department, plus unique views from individual employees.

For example, colleagues working in the admissions department of a clinic or in a home care department may see customers as more interested in health care treatment costs, billing, or scheduling issues. Once these concerns are addressed, other staff may find that the patient becomes more relaxed and focused on his treatment plans and medications.

Customers first want to locate someone who understands their needs, and then they often focus their attention on more pressing health care needs. You will notice that each of the professionals involved in the continuum of care or service delivery process will have a different understanding of what the customer needs.

Make membership on the committee a short-term obligation. Asking staff to participate for only six months or a year will require a minimal time commitment, so the committee member can approach the task without feeling overwhelmed by yet another responsibility. It will also allow you to rotate members periodically, adding new members with fresh ideas for improving the operation. Do not replace all the committee members at once. You want to ensure some continuity.

4. Keep your meetings productive.

Plan your meetings for not more than once or twice a month. People become annoyed with too many regular meetings, and you will soon find fewer and fewer attendees. Take time to develop an agenda and distribute it before the meeting. To keep everyone engaged, also solicit agenda items from committee members. This may help bring items to the surface of which you were unaware. Decide on a regular place to meet and avoid changing locations and confusing your members. Develop a consistent system for delivering meeting notices. The focus of all meetings must be on the customer. The purpose is to examine all interactions with the customer and to identify negative and positive implications for your business. If the outcome of a proposed action is either negative or even just neutral, with no net gain to the customer, then you must reassess it altogether. If your customer would not give you credit for doing something, why do it?

5. Solicit employee feedback.

Before you develop any standards, survey or interview your colleagues. Find out what they know or understand about customer problems and complaints. Frequently employees are the first to become aware of important customer concerns, but have failed to note them. They often do not share this information unless it is requested. They may feel no one respects their opinions or advice. They quietly do their work, leaving the task of solving customer problems to others. The problems that cause a patient or consumer to become angry seldom disappear unless you do something to correct the situation.

You cannot afford to keep the problems hidden. The longer the problem persists the more serious it becomes. It is important for staff members to report all customer service problems to the committee. Fellow employees should be providing the information that guides the committee's work. Employee feedback and input is vital to ensuring that you are addressing real-life issues that you know are important rather than just those you think are important.

6. Set customer service standards.

Begin setting standards that can be measured, observed, or monitored. Define these standards while keeping in mind what you know about customer expectations. For example, decide how many times the telephone should ring before it is answered. Base your standards on customer feedback and what you know your customer values—not on what you as the provider think. The two viewpoints are often different, and if you wish to be customer-focused you must design your service standards according to what the customer values.

Start today by structuring a questionnaire designed to get the maximum feedback around some specific areas of interest for your organization, and then go about setting your office standards. Consider the following examples:

- all telephone calls to be answered by the third ring;

- all requests for brochures or educational materials to be filled the same day as requested;

- all messages receive a response within six hours;

- all telephone messages dated, timed, and signed;

- all employees answer the telephone in exactly the same manner;

- no one promises services/products without first verifying that the product is available; and

- all people making outside appointments/visits must use a checklist to meet objectives during the appointment.

Begin thinking about customer service standards you think should be instituted in your company and then ask your key customers some targeted questions to see how they feel about your ideas. Describe behaviors or tasks you can monitor. You will need to have a system for determining if a task has been completed, as you must be able to observe and measure performance. Do you have any ideas for behaviors to measure?

Recommendations for Customer Service Standards

1. _____

2. _____

3. _____

4. _____

5. _____

7. Start off with training.

When the standards are developed, create and schedule training meetings to discuss implementation procedures. Highlight any problems that could occur in the initiation process. Training will help staff recognize the value of the program and its potential for improving the business operation. Every standard should have a reason for existence and everyone should know the rationale. Prior to implementation, new standards or policies should be discussed, reviewed, and analyzed. People are more apt to follow new rules when they understand what they mean, have contributed to the development of the policy, and can anticipate a positive outcome. Management should project how the new standards will contribute to the business. The purpose of the program is to make your business more efficient, customer oriented, and profitable.

Follow these simple guidelines: (1) Get specific customer feedback, (2) write the customer service policy, (3) teach and inform everyone about the policy, (4) monitor the use of the policy, (5) determine the effectiveness of the policy, (6) modify and alter the policy, and (7) rewrite the policy and begin again to teach the organization about the changes. You will also need to establish a program to reward employees for demonstrating specific behaviors and adhering to the systems. What gets rewarded gets done.

8. Test the process.

Start testing to verify the standards are being met. For example, call your office to see how long it takes for a telephone call to be answered. Ask staff to document when a product is in stock or how a report was distributed. Keep track of all customer mailings, noting the date the customer requested a brochure and the date it was sent. Keep spying on the process. Check with the customer to see if she received what she requested. Constantly monitor your activities to ensure continuous improvements.

Suggestions for Monitoring Customer Service

1. _____

2. _____

3. _____

4. _____

9. Maintain documentation.

The customer service committee should maintain a log of all problems, complaints, and compliments that are registered. It is imperative to never forget, misplace, or disregard a complaint. No complaint, or compliment, is unimportant—all feedback is worthwhile, even if on occasion it is painful to hear. And compliments given to service personnel are an important part of building and maintaining motivation to adhere to service standards.

When a problem occurs, you need to consider not only the incident in question, but how it will affect your business and your reputation. Each problem should receive your careful attention and be discussed individually with those most directly involved.

Just one small customer service error can create additional problems in other areas of the company. For example, if you mistakenly send a client the wrong bill, you have not only shared confidential information but also delayed payment. You may now have the customer talking about your inefficiency, something you want to avoid. He may infer that your inefficiency getting bills to the right address may also be indicative of your inability to provide quality care. And the inferences can go on and on. Review all of your standards and customer issues regarding them. Errors are costly and you do not want to be fueling your competition by internal disorganization.

10. Make adjustments and retrain your colleagues.

Do not become attached to any of your customer service standards. No matter who wrote them, how much time it took to develop the policy, or how well you believe you tested procedures, if they are not working, refine and rewrite them. Get regular and ongoing customer feedback to determine the effectiveness of the standards. If the customers don't value them anymore or your measure of effectiveness has changed, then adjust the standards based on the new feedback. If the standards do not improve your operation, you have not accomplished anything. Why can't you mail the information today? Why can't a customer receive a response within 24 hours? Why are you always at meetings when customers need your help? Policies that do not make it easier for customers to do business with your company make customers go away.

1. What is the purpose of a customer service program?

_____

_____

_____

_____

2. Name some of the qualities you should look for in a program leader.

_____

_____

_____

_____

3. Who should be asked to serve on a customer service committee?

_____

_____

_____

_____

4. How should you structure customer service committee meetings?

_____

_____

_____

_____

5. Why is customer feedback important in setting standards for service?

_____

_____

_____

15

Building a Customer Service Team That Works

Objectives

- Define the meaning of a team.
- Learn strategies for team building.
- Identify team players and roles.

Very few services or products in the health care industry can be delivered through the efforts of only one person. Fulfilling customer requests often involves several people to take the order, do the research, prepare the report or product for delivery, or gather the data requested. One person answers the telephone and then transfers the call to the appropriate person in another department. Customers who contact your office may have to go through several layers before they reach the right person.

For the timely coordination of services, it is important to develop an efficient team. Good teamwork is integral to the delivery of quality customer service. How do we create a productive team? Let's start by defining what we mean.

Teams are comprised of a number of people associated with a work unit or activity. Each member of the team has a unique personality and skill set. The group can include people with varied backgrounds, different agendas, and a multitude of talents. To tap the skills of team members for the benefit of customers, we should make an effort to get to know our colleagues. What skills do they have? Are they bilingual? Do they know sign language? Are they computer whizzes with dot-com experience who can assist customers on the Internet?

Team building is a process. As the team develops, the services improve and both the organization and the customer win. The process of team building requires the commitment of the managers and employees who form the team and their willingness and ability to make things better for the customer. The team building process allows us to harness the strengths of many people. But first we must identify individual capabilities. Do you have skills that management has yet to realize? Have you thought about additional contributions you could make to benefit the organization?

Developing a quality team takes work. When the team works well, the customer is impressed. Here are some tips for building your team.

- **Adhere to a system**. Maintain consistency in your activities. Have each team member process calls, take orders, handle requests a set way.

- **Evaluate the process.** Look at all aspects of your operation and determine what could make it stronger and more reliable. The customer should be able to expect the same quality of service from any member of the team at any time.

- **Solicit everyone's opinions about the team's work.** Plan regularly scheduled meetings to discuss the service you provide and how the team can be more effective.

- **Test new procedures**. When you develop a new process or system for the team to follow, do it and review it. While the process may look like it is going to work, it is imperative to review and analyze the results. Correct any process that could negatively affect customer relations.

- **Use the word "team" as you interact with your customers**. It is reassuring for the customer to be aware that there is an entire support team in your office to help her. Let her know that you are not the only person who can assist her and that she is fortunate to have other team members to go to for support and advice.

Every team includes a variety of people. Make sure you understand who is on your team and what his function is. Who can you count on when either you or the customer needs additional assistance? Think of your team as a buddy system, people you can rely on when you need them.

Team members include leaders, thinkers, followers, and planners.

Leaders are those who are quick to delegate. While some leaders may have a positive impact on the team, by taking charge and guiding the process, others can diminish team spirit by exhibiting a better-than-you attitude. Effective leaders solicit contributions from their fellow team members. They hold themselves accountable. When they make decisions, they assume responsibility for their actions. They model behaviors that others can emulate and thereby gain support from those they work with.

The **thinkers** are those who seem to make bigger contributions after the meeting is over and often in private. They help others understand the process and where everyone fits in. Sometimes they hold up the process by too much "what if" thinking.

Followers go along with the group without questioning. Unfortunately, they may become aware of customer service problems but do not tell other members of the group so as not to rock the boat. Followers often fail to contribute information needed for decision making. They can be passive-aggressive and actually destroy the path to success. They may take up space within the group but not work with the group.

The **planners** help other members of the team look ahead and build a vision. They help teammates understand what the customer needs even before the actual request comes to our attention. Planners provide visions and options for us to consider as we plan new customer service strategies.

You and Your Team Members: Who's Who?

Who are the leaders on your team? What do they do to help or hurt the team process?

1. _____
2. _____
3. _____

Who are the thinkers on your team? Have they helped you understand the process?

1. _____
2. _____
3. _____

Who are the followers on your team? Do they follow along and make no contributions?

1. _____
2. _____
3. _____

Who are the planners on your team? Do they keep talking about tomorrow?

1. _____
2. _____
3. _____

How would you describe yourself and the type of team member you are?

_____
_____

Some team participants create roadblocks in the development of any new service or program. They are often called **resisters**. They oppose change and can be uncooperative. They nod their heads in agreement and then do nothing to help or move the process along. While the team leader tries to bring some of this resistance into the open, resisters prevent this from happening. People often call these members heel draggers. You should be aware of how they work and how they can hurt the operation. They are always asking to put decisions off, requesting programs be piloted first, or shelving issues for later meetings. Do you recognize the type?

Other resister types are mere **antagonists**. They can be very vocal and even annoying in their disagreement of a new service strategy or plan. Arguments do not seem to sway them and they are steadfast in their beliefs. They often tell you it was better where they used to work and have absolutely no understanding of the value of compromise. Found one on your team?

Another type of resister is one who continues to sit on the fence. They never commit to any one issue or cause and refuse to take a stand on an issue. They take long periods of time to make up their minds and seem to be more fearful of hurting someone, than actually doing what is best for the company and the customer. Fence-sitters never let you know what they are actually thinking.

For the team to function at its best, it needs the involvement of all members. Teams need information to make decisions and to develop a customer-driven organization. Teams take time to develop. Get to know the people you work with and learn how to effectively communicate with them. Begin using some of the following strategies:

- Plan some team brainstorming sessions for your organization.

- Schedule sessions to discuss how better to serve your customers.

- Encourage creative thinking and possibly reward new and valuable ideas.

- Break down team barriers. If you find certain members of the team are sitting quietly and not contributing, take it upon yourself to solicit their opinions and ideas. You need help from everyone.

- Do not criticize or discourage contributions. The challenges presented by the health care customer are tremendous and we need all the help we can get. You never know when a gem will surface from all those not-so-good ideas.

My Contributions to the Team

Think about the description of the different team members. What is your role on the team? Have others write descriptions of team members (risky but valuable). Answer the following questions.

What have I contributed to my team?

How can I be a better team member?

Do I usually cause problems or do I solve them? __ I cause them __ I solve them

Explain why.

1. How would you define team?

_____

_____

_____

_____

2. What are some strategies for team building?

_____

_____

_____

_____

3. How can a leader have a positive impact on the team?

_____

_____

_____

_____

4. What role do planners play in team development?

_____

_____

_____

_____

5. How do resisters impede progress?

_____

_____

_____

_____

16

Negotiating With Your Health Care Customer

Objectives

- Define the elements of a winning negotiation.

- Outline the critical factors in the negotiation process.

- Understand how negotiators think.

One of the important strategies for working with customers involves negotiating. Negotiating with customers takes place all the time. We may negotiate with patients regarding the day of their appointments, the best time for a conference call, or the place to have a meeting. Home care companies may have to negotiate when arranging for a nurse to do a patient's dressing change. The medical equipment company may negotiate on the best times to deliver the customer's oxygen.

Many times health care professionals assume they know what is best for the customer and see little need to negotiate. Making assumptions can be a mistake. If we are going to achieve positive outcomes for both our business and our health care consumer, we need to learn how to negotiate. Providers can offer better service when they understand the value of the negotiation process and recognize the importance of reaching agreement with customers on the plan, product, or service to be delivered.

Win-Win Negotiating

Everyone transacting business should understand the goals and objectives of the negotiation process. Needs vary: Your customer may have one objective and you may have another. For example, the customer may want an appointment this week, while you are concerned about filling up an empty calendar next week. You may want to fill the home care nurse's day while she is in the south end of the city, and the patient wants to see the nurse on a day when his son will be in the neighborhood.

In a **win-win negotiation,** you get what you want—and the customer/patient gets what he wants. While it may not be possible for both parties to get everything they asked for, you strive to reach the best compromise. The word "no" is only an opening position for the good negotiator.

What are the three stages of every negotiation?

1. Establish needs. Find out exactly what the customer is looking for. What type of insurance coverage is she interested in? What home care services does she need? Create a list of criteria or goals that each party needs to focus on. When you begin to focus on one issue or goal, you will move closer to meeting the customer's needs and resolving her problems.

2. Get information. Find out all the details. Get the specifics about goals and define in detail the key issues that must be addressed. What, when, and where does she need the service provided? If he needs insurance, whom does he need it for? Have you taken time to learn more about the beneficiaries? Do not jump to conclusions and let previous experiences get in the way of clarifying facts. Whenever people are involved every situation is unique.

3. Strive for a compromise. In most negotiations neither the customer nor the health care provider can get everything he asks for. While you may be able to give the patient an appointment with the physician he prefers, you may not have the requested time or day available in the schedule. Or you may have the desired insurance coverage, but the policy may not allow the policyholder to use the hospital closest to her home. In these initial stages of the negotiation, each person must look for what is most important and return to key criteria developed during the first stage.

What are three critical elements in any negotiation?

The three elements a negotiator juggles deal with power, information, and timing. We start with power. The concepts described below were first introduced by John Wax in an article titled "Power Theory and Institutional Change" appearing in *Social Service Review* (Spring 1971). We are putting Wax's theory into practice in the customer service department.

1. Power. Power is the ability to influence your customer to do what you both agree is best. Power may come from any number of sources including the following:

Legitimate power. This is given to you by your job title. As an assistant manager, clinical director, nursing supervisor, home care manager, or therapist, you will find that people are impressed by your title. It denotes power and experience.

Charismatic power. Your personality can be overwhelming in a negotiation. Personable, friendly, and gracious people can be an attraction for any customer. Consumers may want to deal with people who make conversation and show an interest in them. The sound of your voice, your smile, and apparent control of the situation can be impressive and attractive.

Information power. Your interest in sharing information will help to create a bond between you and the customer. If you become a consultant to the case manager, the physician's office, or the customer and can inform each about terms and details familiar only to those in your particular segment of the health care industry, you can become a valued and trusted customer service partner. Information is power. When you have the information that the other person needs, you hold an enviable position. Make sure you are negotiating with someone who has genuine expertise. An expert on the treatment of diabetes may tell you they are an authority, but you should verify their credentials. A customer who can talk intelligently about his illness and explain clinical details, nevertheless may not fully understand the long-term effects of his medication or what treatments he will need.

2. Information. While it's true that information is power in the hands of an astute negotiator, the real power in any negotiation is what you know about yourself, your business, and your customer. Asking the right questions and probing for pertinent details will increase your ability to meet needs and reach agreements.

3. Timing. Watch your time. Consumers and patients are usually working under time constraints. They often need a service or product to be initiated today or within the near future. If they are no longer employed, they may need individual health insurance. They may require home care nursing for a family member coming to visit or bathtub rails installed before they can take their father home from the hospital. They present a need as well as a time frame in which they want the product or service rendered.

When timing is critical, customers are more often willing to make concessions and compromises. Customers who need documents sent to them by next-day delivery may be willing to pay additional delivery charges, a cost they would not have initially agreed to in the early negotiating stages. Timing is an element affecting almost every issue during the negotiation. Always keep in mind the amount of time in which you have to negotiate. The longer you have, the longer it usually takes.

What are four negotiating styles?

B. Gummer profiled the negotiating styles sketched here in the article "Power, Power, Who's Got the Power" published in *Administration in Social Work* (Vol. 9:2). As you review the following styles, think about your own behavior and decide which profile best describes the way you interact with patients or customers.

The Extroverted. **Extroverts** are people who get overly excited about the entire customer relationship. The problem is they get sidetracked on every issue and have difficulty focusing on the mission. The excitement should be focused on meeting the customer's needs not on the fact that the customer actually called. Extroverts confuse negotiating with making friends and then often fail to help the customer.

The Analytical. Every issue becomes a point for more negotiating. The **analyst** will have you negotiating over what type of policy to buy, how you want to pay, how you want it delivered to your office, when you want to discuss it again, and who in the office you want to be your contact person. People who employ analytical tactics often are very inflexible. They can list the pros and cons for almost any issue. An example would be the nurse who calls the home care company to schedule an appointment for a patient and demands to speak to the same person every time she calls. Another would be a case manager who requests that her patient be seen for physical therapy on the same day and time each week. Change is a stressor that the analytical type will not handle well.

The Amiable. The **amiable negotiator** spends most of the time making sure everyone is happy. While it sounds like a noble strategy, it rarely works. The object becomes not to do what is right, but to please all parties at all times. Making everyone happy does not mean we have been successful at reaching the appropriate goals.

The Pragmatic. In this approach the only thing that counts is getting the negotiation over with and moving on to the next patient or customer. Making the appointment, placing the materials in the mail, handling the next telephone call, or completing the task now is the primary focus of the **pragmatic negotiator.** Making sure that what we are doing is correct, complete, and appropriate becomes secondary. If you take a pragmatic approach to negotiation, you may be doing things to meet your needs rather than those of the customer. Pragmatic negotiators will call customers back to verify information, but their main purpose is to move quickly to the next task.

What is your negotiating style?

- Describe the "extroverted" style. Is this you?

_____

_____

- Are you the "analytical" type? If so, how would you approach negotiations?

_____

_____

- Could be you're really quite "amiable." What would this mean?

_____

_____

- Perhaps you're the "pragmatic" type. Describe yourself.

_____

_____

- Or maybe you're a combination of several negotiating styles. If this is the case, discuss your original approach.

_____

What are the characteristics of a good negotiator?

Good negotiators exhibit certain positive traits. In the sections below the characteristics are named and described. You may want to adopt some of these behaviors as you develop your own negotiating style.

Convey an image of confidence. When working with any patient or customer, it is important for you to appear confident that you can assist them. You can convey this feeling by looking directly in the customer's eyes, standing straight and tall, and even walking with assurance. You also send a message of confidence by speaking clearly and distinctly.

Maintain a spirit of conviction. Believe in the process or program that you are coordinating for the customer. If you do not believe that the insurance policy, medical product, or therapy is right for the customer, it will be difficult to convince the person of its value. You should feel good about representing your company to the customer, or you may be working in the wrong place. If you feel uncertain about your ability to call a customer back at a specific time, this will be evident to the consumer. Your spirit of conviction will be very valuable in reassuring the customer that you will do what was promised.

Work with controlled flexibility. While you may be unable to change corporate policies for each customer, recognize situations that require additional service and bend the rules. Some case managers may want to call you after 6:00 p.m. when your office closes at 5:00 p.m. Some home care patients may need a Sunday delivery. A family needing a new wheelchair for their four-year-old daughter may want to meet with you during evening hours. We are not talking about changing or breaking company rules, just making additional accommodations to retain business.

Maintain endurance. Patients, families, and professional referral sources may need extra time to identify their needs and to understand their options. Forcing them to negotiate under pressure could cost you business. Telling people the contract or deal must be completed today or the offer will expire is a quick way to jeopardize the relationship and lose the contract. You must have patience.

Many social workers, clinical directors, or case managers are handling cases and diagnoses for which they have had little previous experience. Patients may be purchasing long-term care insurance for the first time, having heard about it from a few brief comments on television. A case manager may be handling a patient's reimbursement problems only because their supervisor assigned them the contract that required them to care for this client. You'll need to be patient in your efforts to educate customers and help them become informed decision makers.

Have respect for all involved. Winning negotiators show respect for all the parties involved in the transaction process. Accept that each negotiator is only trying to accomplish what she believes is best for herself and/or her patients. As we've emphasized in previous chapters, customers don't usually fit into one neat category. Some customers may not be well informed. On the other hand, customers can be smarter than you think. Each patient reacts differently to illness. Some case managers handle large caseloads with ease, while others struggle to manage a few cases. Even your professional colleagues can have difficulty understanding terminology that you use on a regular basis. Customize your approach to fit the case in point.

Accept limited victory. You cannot have it all in every negotiation. While you may be able to convince the patient to go to therapy, you may find that she is willing to go only once a week. While you may have convinced the customer to purchase some type of health insurance, she may not find it necessary to extend the coverage to a long list of products that you have suggested. As customers come to realize that you cannot do everything that they suggest, negotiation becomes imperative.

Have product knowledge. You cannot negotiate, modify, or alter your product if you do not fully understand it. If you are arranging for a wheelchair to be delivered to the client's home, you need to understand how the delivery process works. How can you ensure that the chair arrives as scheduled? If you are preparing a written report for a customer, you will need to know what costs you will have to calculate and what approvals you will need before preparing the final document. Do your homework. Read the manual. Make sure you have the answers to all the frequently asked questions.

The Mind of the Negotiator

Before any conversation with a customer you need to consider your abilities to help the customer and to anticipate how the customer may react to your offers. What is the person on the other side of the telephone or table thinking? These strategies will help you understand the mindset of those on either side of the negotiation table.

Never underestimate the intelligence of the parties negotiating. People are often smarter than we give them credit. Provide clearly written product descriptions and instructions. Respect your customer's ability to pay attention, understand, and learn. You will be surprised by your customer's ability to grasp the details and make informed decisions.

Be prepared to give, add, and take away. Families often realize that for a better or more improved product they will have to pay more. Patients accept that seeing a preferred physician may require an extra long wait. You would hope, too, that a person seeking your rapid response to a managed care proposal will understand that you may have to spend many hours reviewing financial reports and take more time than originally planned. You may have to negotiate for some additional time if you want to guarantee the quality of the product.

Understand that people do business with people they like. This is a key concept that permeates this entire text. No one wants to continue a relationship with a clinician, health insurance company, case manager, or hospital in which they feel unwelcome, humiliated, or pressured.

Understand that you cannot be the only winner. The person you are speaking with must be allowed to keep her own dignity and to have some power over her situation. You cannot keep telling people the exact times they need to call you or the exact times they need to be at their appointments. Give them some room in the negotiation. Customers need to have some control over their lives and you must compromise whenever possible.

Strategies for Winning the Negotiation

If the ultimate goals are to be achieved and needs are to be met, you will want to put these tips into practice.

Locate the decision maker. Few patients come to you without some type of support system. You may want to speak to those who are advising your customer. Family members, caregivers, parents, or a case manager may be included on this list. They may be extremely important in the process of reaching the right outcome. They may actually be the customer's real decision maker.

Read the organizational chart. If you going to be working with a hospital, clinic or physician's office, you may want to request an organizational chart. The chart will help you understand who makes decisions for specific products and with whom you need to speak when particular problems occur. When an organizational chart is not available, you will want to begin creating your own so that you can understand the organizational structure.

Realize the existence of hidden agendas. Do not be consumed with all the "whys" in any negotiation. For example, why the family must have the appointment only on Friday or why they want to talk only to Susan in the billing department. If you are focused on all the hidden agendas, it is difficult to move the process toward solving the customer's problems.

What are the six components of a winning deal?

1. Each party receives what it expected. Agreeing on what to expect and then to see it actually happen makes everyone happy. When the case manager expects you to call at 2:00 p.m. and you do, you are on your way to a positive business relationship. Making good on the service you promised is the very best advertisement for repeat business.

2. Everyone understands the rewards. No one wants surprises, especially when it comes to health care. If the policy doesn't offer the mental health benefits the policyholder expected, you have an unhappy customer. When the packet of materials or the product in the box is exactly what was promised, everyone wins.

Take time to tell the customer about all the paperwork that he will be receiving, the color of the wheelchair, or the name of the home care nurse coming to change his dressing. It's best to close all the information gaps.

3. Everyone feels like a winner. When people receive a quality product for what they believe is a fair price, they are pleased and satisfied. Stroke your customer's ego and make her feel like a winner. Always treat her with respect, intelligence, and honesty.

4. There is an escape clause. Any good business arrangement needs to have an escape clause. If the insurance policy or the company representing the product does not provide the service the customer expects, the customer must be able to terminate the relationship. The patient should not have to continue receiving his home oxygen from a company that is not responsive. If a physician or home care company neglects to return telephone calls, again, the patient should be able to sever ties. Put a written guarantee behind your products and always make it clear that no relationship is ongoing unless requested by the consumer.

5. All questions have been answered. The deal is only a good one when the agreement is clear. People should always be offered time to ask questions and receive clear, accurate answers, and never be rushed to make a decision. Questions should also be encouraged once the agreement has been made, offering opportunities for further refinement of the arrangement.

6. Parties are willing to do it again. The best outcome of any negotiation process is when the customer says, "I want to do business with you again." You know you have done well when the hospital-based case manager says, "I want to refer another patient to you" or when a customer comments that she wants to purchase another health care policy from your company. Having repeat business is your best outcome and more important than any letter of recommendation.

Successful outcomes in negotiating happen when the customer, family, or referral sources receive what they want and you receive what you want. For you the best result of your negotiation will come in the form of a well-respected reputation, fair financial remuneration, and the opportunity to continue in a successful business.

Negotiation is Not Always a Smooth Course

There can be pitfalls. Always be aware of the more unusual tactics negotiating parties employ. And watch out for the self-induced traps. Consider these strategies to overcome snags in the process.

Asking for more than is expected. In the initial negotiation, patients often begin requesting more than they know they can expect. The home care client wants the nurse to stay longer hours or to come to the house more frequently. He may request reduced fees for paying in cash or ordering products in large quantities. Sometimes the customer is successful in his attempts to get more than the norm. Is there something the customer can do to get you to do more?

Threatening it will cost you business if demands are not met. A patient may tell you that if you do provide the service or take care of her needs, she will report the story to the media or call her physician. Be careful about how you respond to threats. You need to maintain your ethics and sound business practices in spite of demanding customers.

Setting aside your critical issues and concentrating on the most important one. Do not avoid addressing issues critical to the patient or customer. If the customer has a primary issue he wants to discuss, handle it first. Often he is so focused on one issue that he hears nothing until you address what is most important to him. If the first question concerns having an oncology nurse work with his mother, this may be the first issue you need to talk about. If the customer is looking for home care insurance that is available in her hometown, she will want this issue addressed before she is even willing to share her name with you. The customer's critical issue may not be the same as yours.

Talking too wise or acting too smart. Talking about all the years you have worked in the health care industry and why you know what is best for the customer may not be acceptable. Just present facts, statistics, and research to back your recommendations. You don't want to overwhelm your customers with your superior knowledge. Keep them focused on the product or service—not on your impressive achievements.

Believing only what we see in writing. You may need to put the treatment plan, numbers, dates, and appointments in writing. If you have negotiated a plan with the patient, write it down. It will provide the customer additional security by knowing what he can expect. When the customer is able to see a written summary of the costs, he will have a clearer understanding of the numbers. Many people believe only what they see in writing. By writing out your plan or proposal, you will move closer to reaching agreement. It's easier when everyone is looking at the very same document.

Negotiating and providing quality customer service happens at the same time. Customer service requires multiple interactions. It involves reaching an agreement about goals. You cannot avoid negotiating. Look over this chapter again and decide which negotiating strategies you have used. Have you discovered the strategies that work best in your work setting? You will soon find that with the right negotiation skills your list of winners will be endless.

Review Questions

1. How would you define win-win negotiating?

   _____

   _____

   _____

   _____

2. What are three stages in the negotiating process?

   _____

   _____

   _____

   _____

3. How do you derive power or the ability to influence others?

   _____

   _____

   _____

   _____

4. List and describe the characteristics of an effective negotiator.

   _____

   _____

   _____

   _____

5. What are the six components of a winning deal?

   _____

   _____

   _____

   _____

17

Creating Efficiency in Your Health Care Business Environment

Objectives

- Define the goals for improving efficiency.

- Recognize the value of keeping records current and organized.

- Learn how to do it right the first time.

Customers constantly challenge our ability to react in a timely and professional manner. Can you respond rapidly to a customer's request for information? Are you prepared to describe an insurance policy so that the customer will have a clear understanding of its provisions and benefits? How quickly can you locate the documents a client recently sent you? The test of your efficiency and systems never ends.

Designing an efficient and productive workplace will enhance the service you deliver. Efficiency saves you time, money, and manpower. It's like a savings account. When you save time by streamlining your operation, you're really saving money for your organization AND you're creating an environment with less stress. Management has most of us working with a large customer base, including organizations, facilities, professionals, patients, and clients with a lot of needs, requests, and problems for us to solve. To increase your business and keep your customers happy, efficiency becomes a necessity.

One goal for any operationally efficient person or organization is to avoid needless repetitive actions, pitfalls/problems, and complaints. The ability to rapidly locate information and to have immediate access to important data allows you to quickly assist the customer in making the right decisions. Here are steps you can take to create greater efficiency in your workplace.

Attack the large mound of paper and files.

Take a look at those overstuffed file cabinets, the piles of paper on your desk waiting for an organized home, and the hundreds of documents stored on your computer. What materials can you box and send to the warehouse? What documents are you saving on your computer, knowing too well that you will never look at them again? Have you found that you have more than one file for a client/account and do not understand the reason why? The first step to a more efficient you is getting rid of the clutter.

Consider a coding system for easier identification of files.

When you are organized and have quick access to all the essential records, you are poised and ready to offer your customer a rapid response. Consider placing a front sheet in each file identifying its contents. You may also want to update this document continually, adding current information. Locating customer records is easier when you're organized. You can color code files by account, specialty, contract, or any other segment. The idea is to shorten the time it takes to locate information for yourself and the customer.

Review and contact business associates and customers for updated information.

As providers of health care goods and service, we are continually called on to inform and help clients access assistance throughout the industry, and we need quick-look resources at our fingertips. Take time to update your address book or Rolodex of frequently called national, regional, and local community referral sources. Identify new contact people, telephone numbers, addresses, and e-mail addresses that you refer to on a regular basis. You may want to develop a master list of resources that can be shared with others in your office. Make sure you are continually adding new and important names to the list and deleting those you no longer need or ones that may have changed. Create a special list of names and numbers for those most frequently contacted. Always keep your directories handy so you can look up telephone numbers while you have the customer on the phone and avoid having to call them back.

When developing this list, ask for input from other members of your staff. The list should include all numbers frequently used by most members of your health care team. Post and distribute the list. Make copies for everyone who may need it.

Developing a Contact List

When was the last time you updated your business telephone list?

What are the 10 telephone numbers you most need on your desk?

Who will you ask to help you develop this contact list?

Who should receive the list?

Ensure your ability to access information quickly.

While it is wonderful to know you have the information that the customer needs, it is terribly frustrating when you are unable to access it. You could be searching for information on utilization management, outcomes, schedules of meetings, or just a telephone number. Whatever the source, if the data were available on your computer and you knew how to use the technology to access it quickly, you would be more efficient. If current information that you supplied was to be entered into your computer database and it has not been, why not? You do not want to be operating your business with outdated information and incorrect numbers. Who in your office is in charge of database administration?

Dedicate yourself to doing it right the first time.

If you want to be efficient and improve your work efforts—slow down! Take time to review all of your work carefully. Work from a plan. This allows you time to carefully review all of your written reports, letters, and assessments. Time wasted in doing tasks more than once leads to frustration and often to a lack of enthusiasm for the project and for helping the customer. It is also valuable to have a colleague review your work before you submit a report or proposal for final approval.

When speaking with the customer, gather information completely and thoroughly the first time. If you are traveling to an appointment, obtain clear and detailed directions. Do not count on your sense of just knowing where you are going. Verify all appointments, times, and spelling of names. You want to avoid having to call customers back to ask questions and obtain information you should have correctly and completely received during the first phone call. Treasure your time and the customer's. From the simplest task to the most complex operating system, there are ways you can improve, become more efficient, and provide the customer with service that puts you a notch above the competition.

Being efficient has a lot to do with developing new habits. Condition your customer to expect the best!

Review Questions

1. What tasks can you tackle to make yourself more efficient?

   _____

   _____

   _____

   _____

2. How can you achieve the goal of "doing it right the first time"?

   _____

   _____

   _____

   _____

18

The Management Challenge: Hiring Right and for the Right Reasons

Objectives

- Develop effective strategies for recruiting and hiring.

- Identify resources for attracting prospective employees.

- Evaluate job qualifications.

Managers and supervisors are continually faced with the challenge of hiring the right people. Making hiring decisions is complex and stressful. Yet quality service is dependent on placing the right person in the right position. No one wants to deal with an employee who is unhappy with his work and responsibilities—least of all your customers!

As a manager, you want to avoid employee turnover. Excessive churning creates work-related stress on employees who remain with the organization and must take on additional job responsibilities until a replacement is hired. You may be pressured by your own manager as well as subordinates to fill a vacancy quickly. But before you jump the gun on hiring someone, consider the impact of hiring the wrong person.

First, you need to be patient. Finding the right person takes time and work. Jobs in customer service call for "people" skills. Not everyone wants to interact with the public. You can start by looking within your organization for people who may have the patience and the stamina to work with the public. If you can get a referral from a friend or colleague, you're in luck. However, just because a prospect comes with a personal recommendation does not guarantee that she is the perfect candidate for dealing with customers.

Evaluate your needs. At the onset of the recruitment process, decide if hiring a full-time employee is the answer. Often part-time employees can very effectively fill the position. If you want the customer to be able to reach a representative throughout the day, then full-time workers may be the only option. Don't overlook other opportunities. There are excellent employees available if you are willing to create flexible work schedules. Better to have a pleasant, efficient person working part time, than an angry short-tempered employee working full time. And part-time employees can cost you less because you may not have to offer them a full benefits package.

How to Find the Right Person

There are many ways to find good employees, and you should explore all your options. For starters, ask yourself who delivers the best customer service in your company? How and where did management locate these employees? You may need to return to that source once again.

Getting a person who's a good fit for the job makes the effort worthwhile. Don't forget your customers are at stake. Although the recruitment process can become costly, especially classified advertising, there are numerous approaches you can take, including:

- placing an advertisement in the newspaper,

- networking and talking with colleagues,

- advertising in professional newsletters or journals,

- posting openings in your office,

- posting openings on your website,

- obtaining referrals from present employees, and

- hiring former employees.

Once the recruiting is underway, you'll start receiving letters and resumes. The sections that follow describe qualifications to look for as you begin your selection process.

Experience. Determine what the job applicant knows and what she has learned from past work settings. Determine if her past experiences will allow her to become an effective and respected company representative.

Skill set. What are his skills? What are his areas of expertise? Has he had experience dealing with patients and stressed customers?

Growth potential. Assess the candidate's ability to learn and to grow professionally. While it is important to bring certain skills and experiences to the new position, hire people who want to learn about new programs and grow personally and professionally.

Team player. Will this person be a good fit? Does the applicant appear so attached to the ways of former employers that she shows little interest in working with your team? Does she keep talking about her former employer as the ultimate in service or product? Do you think she will be able to adapt to your work environment?

Goal-oriented. Look for people who aspire to do and be more than they are today. You want to hire people who strive to achieve career goals. Everyone in the office will benefit from people who are motivated to excel.

Flexibility. Many companies have offices in various parts of the city or throughout the country, located in different time zones. Customers may come from different cultural backgrounds. You'll want to hire someone who is comfortable working with a variety of people and can adapt well to each situation.

Positive attitude. You want customer friendly people who can offer consistent service at all levels. Customers include professionals calling on behalf of their clients as well as end-users of products and services calling for themselves. Each brings to the relationship a unique set of stressors. You want to employ people who are enthusiastic and motivated, and who care about the results of their interactions with customers.

Creative. Seek individuals who can think creatively and are not afraid to offer their ideas for solving customer problems or improving service. New technology, advertising, innovative programs and products have all influenced customers and made them more aware of what is available and what they can expect from you. Employees need to be willing to change directions, to go the extra mile to win over the customer. This means being ready to handle requests for services that go beyond the routine.

Effective communicator. You must look for employees who have outstanding oral and written skills. You need to ask each prospective employee to write a short paragraph explaining the details of a customer complaint that they handled. If the job candidate demonstrates poor writing or verbal abilities, you may want to place his application on the bottom of the pile.

Innovative. Search for someone who is looking for something new. Ties to tradition may not work now. The health care industry advances rapidly. Today's consumers are more knowledgeable. Consequently, customer service providers need to be up-to-date and enjoy the excitement of new developments.

How to Avoid Hiring the Wrong Person

You may be an astute judge when it comes to selecting the perfect person for the job. Whether you base your hiring decision on gut instinct or a careful analysis of qualifications, there are a few red flags to watch for. Here are some words of caution about hiring people for the wrong reasons. You'll want to avoid hiring people who...

... claim they know all the right people and have all the right connections. These overzealous folks are often no better at solving problems than the person who is new to the industry but is dedicated to helping the customers. You do not want

people who claim to have all the answers. Instead consider those who are willing to take time to locate the answers. Hire good people who can do the job with dedication and commitment. Your customers will quickly get to know these people and seek them out when they have a problem.

. . . promise your customer problems will go away once they arrive. Getting and keeping business takes time and a great deal of effort. Be careful about job seekers who make dramatic promises to alter your business image in a matter of weeks. Relationships take time to be tested and the customer needs time to build confidence in your business. It can be a slow process and employees need to remain consistent in their efforts to provide quality service.

. . . change jobs because they knew more than their previous boss. They may also leave your company once they realize they know more than you. They are easy to spot by their know-it-all attitude. They refer to previous bosses as idiots and colleagues as incompetent. Their resumé reflects a poor work history, and they cite poor management that failed to listen to their advice as the reason they left.

. . . always wanted to work for your company or you personally. Doesn't everyone want to work for you? While this sounds good, be careful. This is not enough reason to offer them a job. Your customer needs more than the employee's dedication to the employer. Once you recover from the flattery and the outlandish display of affection, take a look at the reality of the situation and what will be best for the company, you, and the customer.

. . . say they need to work somewhere. Great! What dedication to themselves and their profession. While it may be true that they need a job, it is not something you want to hear repeated to your customers. Anyone who just needs a place to work, and tells you that, might not be the person you want working with your customers.

. . . do not need the money. That may sound okay, but it is unreal. Everyone cares about the money. Everyone is either paying bills or saving for the future. Wait until you offer her half of what everyone else is earning doing the same work and then see if she still wants the job. Hire people who need the cash, want to work, and are eager to do what is right for the customer and to maintain employment.

. . . are working only to give themselves something to do. Do not hire people who are lonely, bored, or simply looking for a place to fill their day. The position you are filling requires professional commitment and not someone seeking a hobby.

. . . keep asking about the work hours, breaks, and vacation time. Look for the employee who is focused on the position, its challenges and responsibilities. You want to hear remarks about what he can do to be successful and questions concerning your goals for customer service, not about time off and vacations.

When interviewing prospective employees, be careful about the questions you ask. Seek legal advice or have human resources guide you through the hiring process. Many topics should be avoided, including but not limited to: age/date of birth, birthplace, previous address, religion/race, mother's surname, marital status, maiden name, number of children, who will care for them while they are working, prior workman's compensation claims, membership in any social organization, arrests, or past injuries or diseases.

Do your homework when you prepare for the employment interview. There is much to learn regarding appropriate interview techniques. Again, the human resources department can assist you. Knowing where to search for applicants, reviewing resumés, interviewing, and selecting a candidate can be a long and arduous process. That's why it's important to do it right. A new hire affects the morale of other employees in the department. Service can suffer. Hiring someone who terminates employment after a few months can set back the entire organization. In a nutshell, hiring wrong can be a costly mistake. Getting the right person who's a good match for your department, makes the whole team happy—and your customers, too.

Many times people accept a position only to find they are unhappy with the work required. Managers need to be open to employees expressing concern about their ability to successfully continue in their position. Stress can become unbearable for some employees, affecting job performance and the service the customer receives. For many reasons, attitudes toward a job may change. As a supervisor or manager you must make employees feel comfortable coming to you with their concerns. For the mental health of your colleagues and the continued success of your business, you may need to consider making changes in job responsibilities. Your customers and staff will be very appreciative of your sensitivity.

Evaluating My Own Job

Why did I originally accept this position?

Am I ready for a change?

Think of a time when you hired the wrong person for the job. Why did this happen?

The next person hired to do what I do should have the following characteristics:

1. _____

2. _____

3. _____

4. _____

Review Questions

1. What is the best place to look for job candidates?

   _____
   _____
   _____
   _____

2. Where can you announce job openings?

   _____
   _____
   _____
   _____

3. What qualifications should you screen for?

   _____
   _____
   _____
   _____

4. How can you spot a potential hiring mistake?

   _____
   _____
   _____
   _____

5. Who should you contact for guidance on recruiting and hiring?

   _____
   _____
   _____
   _____

19

Developing a Customer Service Training Program

Objectives

- Understand objectives for promoting customer service training.

- Outline steps for creating a training program.

- Recognize the value of maintaining training records.

- Review a sample training record.

As a topic, customer service training is somewhat like the weather—everybody discusses it but no one thinks they can do anything about it. No matter how you feel about customer service, it is often the hot topic when companies attempt to analyze how and why they lost business. What managers fail to realize is that they can do a great deal to improve the service that they provide, and training employees plays a big part. But the training must reach all levels and areas of the organization. Every employee must be required to attend customer service training sessions.

In developing any health care business unit, managers spend hundreds of hours developing a business plan, creating a budget, structuring a strategic marketing plan, and analyzing the potential market. We know how to create a viable, profitable organization. In business school and from on-the-job experience, we have learned how to negotiate a contract, write a company brochure, and develop strategies for penetrating the marketplace. We know how to obtain the necessary funding, analyze potential business alliances, and determine staffing needs for running an effective operation. Sad to say in all this preparation, we often neglect the most important area of our business—customer service. Possibly we forget about customer service because it's an intangible. It's not something in black and white, a report that can be read or presented to the board of directors.

Most people believe they have done enough work to ensure business success and quickly show you the stacks of paper that outline the strategic plan. They fully believe that the mounds of paper, the budgets and plans that they have produced pave the way to success. *Wrong—very wrong!* It's the people in your organization who will make or break your enterprise.

People do business with people, and no company can be successful without dedicating a tremendous effort to establishing an outstanding customer-driven organization. Ineffective, uncaring, and inefficient people will destroy all the work completed in the preparation of a comprehensive budget or in obtaining and developing a wide selection of products or services for your customers. Your organization will self-destruct unless you prepare your employees for delivering outstanding service.

Developing service strategies tailored to fit your customers is your insurance for surviving and thriving in a competitive health care marketplace. Customer service training must not be an additional segment in your training program, but an educational endeavor that binds together all the facets of your company. You are in business to serve the customer. Your training program should impart this message to everyone who is a part of your enterprise—not just to one or two departments that constitute your customer service front line.

Promote commitment to customer service at all levels of the organization.

Often improving customer service is the goal of only one or two staff people. These are the ones who initiate the first companywide customer service training program. One person is a start, but not enough. With some degree of assertiveness and commitment, the pioneers who champion the cause can be the impetus for moving the program along and attracting support from all levels of the organization, so vital to ensuring success.

Management must be supportive of all components of the training. Start with your senior executives and get them on board for resources—both budget and staff. From there, support will cascade down to department heads, middle managers, and supervisors who can jump on the band wagon by attending training sessions themselves and setting up employee training throughout the organization. Attendance should be required. Meet with your leaders today to promote the importance of quality service. You need their commitment for the success of the program and your organization.

Develop a training manual for your program.

A manual already exists that was tailor-made to meet your needs. Use *Customer Service Strategies for the Health Care Environment* as the focus of your training program. Each chapter or section of this book can be used for an individual in-service training module. Take one section at a time. The study exercises can guide your discussions and help you address issues that will make your company more responsive to meeting the needs of your customers. Each section should be reviewed and analyzed according to how it relates to your business or department.

Follow these steps for designing customer service training sessions.

Listed below are some practical guidelines for structuring your customer service training. Review and follow these steps when creating your own program.

- Require everyone to attend.

- Have the training initiative launched by a leader who has enthusiasm and dedication to the program.

- Make sure management is committed to the program. Require one manager or director to be in attendance at each session.

- Always allow time during the training session for participants to review strategies and comment on applications to specific customer issues or problems.

- Throughout the program allow time for employees to make suggestions for improving service. We need to learn from the experience of others.

- Present the sessions at convenient times so that everyone can attend. Several sessions may need to be scheduled to reach the entire staff.

- During training, review actual customer complaints and discuss how problems could be effectively solved. Prior to attending the session, ask staff to bring with them examples of customer problems and complaints.

- Review the results of the training. By surveying customers, calling your own office, and developing customer focus groups you will learn how well you are doing. Let the employees tell you what they think about the sessions and how the programs have influenced their work or awareness of customer service issues. Get constant feedback from fellow employees.

- Keep up the reminders. Many of us forget about what is important and need reminders about the impact of quality service. We cannot afford to provide anything but outstanding service.

Maintain employee training records.

Maintain a training record for each employee. This will help trainers or supervisors document what employees have learned and also help determine what programs should be developed for the future. Programs may be needed for continuing education certification, licensure, and accreditation. The gaps in staff education become noticeable when you review training records.

Records should be complete and accurate. The record is also important for managers and supervisors to review when they prepare biannual or annual employee evaluations. The record shows which employees participated in training programs and which ones disregarded invitations or requirements to attend. By reviewing the training records, you note the employee's commitment to his work and himself as it is reflected in his willingness to attend educational seminars, especially those that are not mandatory.

Figure 19.1 Sample Employee Training Record

Employee Training Documentation Form

Topic or title of training session: _____

Purpose of the training: _____

Major topics addressed (attach brochure or outline):

_____

_____

Date of training session: _____ Location: _____

Length of program: _____

Were CEUs provided for this program? __ Yes __ No

Did you need CEUs for this program? __ Yes __ No

Presenter(s): _____

_____

Signature of Employee: _____

Department: _____ Date: _____

(Complete this form after attending any customer service training program, conference, or workshop. This will be maintained in your employee record.)

Document programs that were held in your office as well as seminars and conferences held outside your company. It is interesting to see how few people are willing or motivated to go to meetings that require them to move their car or leave their office.

Figure 19.1 shows an Employee Training Documentation Form. The form includes some of the items you should record, but you should customize it to add other materials that you may need for your office. You may want to ask the employee to attach to the form a copy of the brochure for the meeting or a more detailed outline of the program.

Invite employee feedback.

When an employee has completed customer service training, talked about the issues, and evaluated your company's strategies for solving customer complaints, ask for her feedback.

Employees have work experiences and customer service stories to share with colleagues. They have seen and experienced customers and the work environment up close. Their

Figure 19.2   Employee Survey Questionnaire

Areas for Customer Service Improvement

What are the three most important areas in which my company can improve our service?

1. _____

2. _____

3. _____

What are the services that are most important to our customers?

1. _____

2. _____

3. _____

Identify three ways that I can improve and make a difference in the business.

1. _____

2. _____

3. _____

Identify three ways the company can improve the service?

1. _____

2. _____

3. _____

What should we do first to improve the service we provide? _____

---

comments and insight are valuable—not just for enhancing training but also for developing new strategies for customer service and replacing policies that are no longer working.

Figure 19.2 provides a model for developing an employee survey form. You can use the form as a template, customizing the questionnaire to make it relevant to your operation. The conclusion of a training program is a good time to get feedback from employees. Invite participants to complete the survey questionnaire.

While the individual surveys should be considered confidential, you can compile and report data without revealing sources and share overall results with other members of your organization. You may spot some interesting insights and trends. Use the results to enhance future in-service training, for discussion at staff meetings, and as you consider improvements to existing customer service programs.

Review Questions

1. What do you need before you launch a customer service training program?

   _____
   _____
   _____
   _____

2. What materials can you use as content for your training sessions?

   _____
   _____
   _____
   _____

3. Describe steps to take in the creation of a training program.

   _____
   _____
   _____
   _____

4. Why should you maintain employee training records?

   _____
   _____
   _____
   _____

5. What is the purpose for asking employees to complete a survey questionnaire?

   _____
   _____
   _____
   _____

PART FIVE

Handling Customer Complaints

20

The Impact of a Complaint

Objectives

- Explain why customer complaints should be taken seriously.

- Understand the impact of every complaint.

- Describe the costs related to losing a customer.

In the book *Service America*, authors Karl Albrecht and Ron Zemke put some very high price tags on customer loyalty. Examples cited include the automobile industry's estimate that a loyal customer is worth $140,000 over a lifetime. With this sum in mind, isn't it silly for a car dealer to fight over a $20 repair bill or a $5 replacement part? In appliance manufacturing, brand loyalty translates into $2,800 over a 21-year period. And your local supermarkets count on about $4,000 a year per average household.

Customer loyalty is also important in the health care business. Look at the home care industry, for example, where providers' pricing and products are similar. Good service creates loyal customers, who start out needing a small item, possibly a cane, and keep coming back for additional equipment or services. If you treat them right, many people will remain your customers for years. You want to cultivate professional colleagues as customers, too, for they refer people who need your products. Keep in touch with your business associates. They may change positions often, but they usually remain in the industry and can continue to be an excellent source of referrals.

Being committed to quality service means making things right for your customer. That's why you need effective strategies for handling complaints. As the industry changes and the customer makes new demands, you will need to do things differently to improve your service systems.

Peter Drucker, best-selling author and management guru, has said we need to "slough off yesterday" and focus every day on what will make a successful business. The time to change and reassess is not when you are in trouble, Drucker said, but while you are successful. The time to reassess your health care business operation is now. Don't wait until customers start complaining about problems. If a company waits until it is marginal, it is usually too late. Once marginality sets in, it is almost impossible to recover market share and reverse the downward trend.

Drucker also noted that over a long period of relative calm every company should evaluate its position in the marketplace and its perceived value in the eyes of its customers in relation to its competitors. Many of the complaints you receive from customers will be because your competition is doing it differently, but not necessarily better.

Another authority, W. Edwards Deming, recognized for his work in quality improvement, once told his followers that although we may know what it costs to fix a problem, we can never fully grasp the financial loss accrued from a complaint or an unhappy customer.

In the following sections you'll find some general statistics to keep in mind as you contemplate what your customers are worth. These findings evolved from a 1992 study conducted by the Technical Assistance Research Programs in Washington, D.C.

For every customer who voices a complaint, there are 26 others who remain silent.

You must be concerned about this silent majority. Although they continue to need your products, these people will quietly begin to take their business to another provider. They may find it easier, more efficient, or even more pleasant to do business with someone else. While the number of customers who complain is few, they may represent many others who refrain from telling you exactly how they feel about your service. You may never become aware of the reasons they have stopped using your services or buying your products or why you are losing business. Beware of the silent majority. You can see why it's important to keep up communication with your customers.

The average angry customer will tell 8 to 16 other people. Over 10 percent will tell more than 20 people.

The voice of the angry consumer is much louder than any customer you continue to satisfy. Angry people rarely keep their thoughts to themselves. They are often eager to share their displeasure and recount all the details as to why they feel they were wrongly treated. They often advise others to take their business elsewhere. Their negative message is delivered without solicitation and can be extremely damaging to the organizational image that you have worked so hard to develop.

Ninety-one percent of unhappy customers will never again purchase goods and services from you.

When a customer walks away and says that she will never purchase from you again, it is often forever! People remain angry for long periods of time, although they often fail to remember what it was that made them so upset. The only thing they do remember is their resolve: "I am never going to use them again." Many former customers are very good at keeping that promise.

If you make a sincere effort to address their complaints, up to 95 percent of your customers will stay with you.

People are usually appreciative of the effort you extend on their behalf. Your willingness to solve their problems is often rewarded with long-term business relationships. Handling complaints effectively is one way you will be tested. You need to show how concerned you are about keeping the customer happy and to make the appropriate amends for your mistakes. Take some extra steps to fix a problem and you may have the customer for life.

It costs about five times as much to attract a new customer as it does to keep the old one.

Before you receive that first request for a service or product, most likely your company has invested in telephone calls, appointments, sales presentations, promotions, travel, and so forth, just to generate a lead. A high cost is associated with attracting new business. Keeping existing customers happy is a lot less costly than locating new ones and replacing lost revenue.

While the health care industry is experiencing an increase in the number of home care patients, there is also a growth spurt in managed care companies and provider organizations. Competition for today's health care patients is fierce. At the same time, providers are facing a potential decrease in reimbursement dollars. The current scenario should make you realize the financial value of every customer and the investment of time and money you had to make to bring that customer on board. No matter what segment of the health care industry you represent, competition is lurking. Don't take your existing customers for granted! During your next staff meeting, address the issues customers most often complain about and be proactive in tackling potential problems.

The Ways a Customer Can Damage Your Business

Identify three ways a customer can negatively impact your business.

1. _____

2. _____

3. _____

Review Questions

1. What is the estimated lifetime worth of a loyal customer according to the automobile industry?

   _____

   _____

   _____

   _____

2. What does Peter Drucker say is the best time to evaluate your business?

   _____

   _____

   _____

   _____

3. Describe some of the findings reported in the Technical Assistance Research study?

   _____

   _____

   _____

   _____

4. Why is it better to keep existing customers satisfied?

   _____

   _____

   _____

   _____

21

The Most Common Complaints

Objectives

- Identify common customer complaints.
- Understand the impact of passing the blame.
- Recognize the source of problems.

While it would be a gigantic task to list all of the complaints we hear in a year's time, if we kept a record by category we would discover that most complaints center on certain issues. Knowing what these issues are can help you prepare to handle them. In the sections below you'll find descriptions of common complaints and tips for resolving issues that you may encounter.

Being Discourteous

You can detect discourtesy by observing the behavior and attitudes of coworkers. How do your colleagues treat each other? How well do they interact with customers? What's their attitude toward office visitors? Discourtesy is usually not reserved for any one particular group. It's nondiscriminatory!

Remember, common courtesies are always in fashion. *Please* and *thank you* are magical words in the health care business—just as powerful as they are in your personal life. Unfortunately, most people who are rude do not realize the negative impact of discourteous behavior on the success of their business. Being objective about your own behavior is difficult. We often have trouble seeing ourselves as others see us. We must be aware of what we say and how we say it. Listen to people talking in your office and see if you can identify behaviors that may drive customers away. Can undesirable practices be changed? Posting reminders about the need for courtesy in key places in your office may help.

Failing to Keep Promises

The clinical supervisor promises that a nurse will be at the customer's home early Sunday morning, and the nurse doesn't show up. Sales representatives make many promises that other staff members in different locations or departments will have to fulfill, but the coordination of services breaks down. The office manager promises a delivery that doesn't happen. A customer service representative promises that a product is in the warehouse, without taking the time to check stock. And the owner of a company may promise anything just to get the business. Make sure you can deliver on your promises. Customers want what they were promised and can be keenly acute at remembering what they were told.

Blaming the System

People become upset when you are unable to take an order due to the failure of the system. Avoid blaming someone else for problems that the customer is experiencing. If the computer is not working, try taking the order with paper and pencil. If the person who handles billing is out of the office, take the request and then get back to the customer with the needed information. Stop talking about fixing blame and start finding the solution.

Passing the Problem to Someone Else

Customers quickly tire of employees passing the buck to someone else. All too frequently customers hear comments like: "It's not my department" or "I don't handle that." Often the first person hearing the problem is anxious to move on to the next customer or call. They make no attempt to assist the customer except to transfer the problem to someone else's desk.

When the customer is anxious to present her problem and find a quick solution, she can become extremely agitated if passed to the next person with the comment, "I'll get someone to help you." Often callers must go through several layers before they get to someone who has the power to solve their problem. What can you do in your organization to reduce the number of people the customer must talk to? In your next staff meeting, discuss this issue with your supervisor and colleagues to see if there are ways you can refine your procedures. Maybe you need to keep the organization directory handy so you can see at a glance who is responsible for what. Whatever you come up with, empathize with the customer. No one likes being put on hold or transferred to three or four people. It's a red flag to the customer that your company is disorganized. In the process of having to wait, many customers lose patience and just hang up the phone and never call back.

Tracing the Source of the Complaint

A large percent of the complaints that you receive usually stem from similar causes or situations. To pinpoint problem areas, you may have to do some investigation. You must develop an understanding of your organizational systems so you can monitor and track down possible glitches. For starters, you can locate many of the sources of complaints or problems by reviewing the following.

- Complaint logs kept in your office
- Letters received from referral sources

- Billing errors

- Credit errors

- Delivery problems (late or even lost drivers)

- Patient records/charts

- Product defects

- Callbacks to customers

- Feedback from sales representatives

- Number of returns or allowances

- Service quality complaints

- Time between complaints and solutions

- In-house suggestions

All of the areas listed above should be monitored on a routine basis to spot problem trends. You may need to collaborate with colleagues in other departments to develop a system for identifying potential problems and to create an action plan to resolve issues. You need to be proactive in problem solving so that you can intercept early on, before a situation mushrooms and causes you to lose customers and business.

You cannot begin to solve problems until you have identified the origin and cause. Is it a people problem, a failure to train staff adequately? Maybe it's a technical error in the information system that you have devised for sending reports to your customers. Learn as much as possible about how your organization operates, the key roles people play, your information systems, billing cycles, delivery procedures, and so forth. The more you know about the intricacies of your operation, the more you can contribute to ensuring your customer's complete satisfaction. Your ability to shepherd your customer through the service sector without a glitch makes you an MVP (most valued player).

Review Questions

1. How can you spot the potential for discourteous behavior among staff?

   _____

   _____

   _____

   _____

2. Besides discourteous behavior, what other issues can aggravate customers?

   _____

   _____

   _____

   _____

3. How can you spot problem trends and become more proactive in finding solutions before you lose customers?

   _____

   _____

   _____

   _____

22

The Value of a Complaint

Objectives

- Understand how complaints can affect company image.

- Identify the positive impact of a complaint.

- Outline what to do when you first hear about a problem.

- Recognize the importance of tracking all complaints.

While complaints are never welcome, they always deserve full attention and must be treated with extreme concern. If you are not receiving any complaints, you have either reached 100 percent perfection or your customers may not be feeling comfortable enough to share their problems with you. Customers may already be taking their business somewhere else. It would be a financial disaster to have business problems and not be aware of them.

Check your customer list to find out who has stopped calling.

Begin by reviewing all of your business records. Look over your list of customers. Check to see how often they call and begin asking about customers from whom you have not heard in a long time. Those who have not called in several months should be your primary concern. Find out why calls have dropped off. Have they moved their business to a new provider? Did they have a complaint? If they did have a complaint, are they sharing this information with other potential customers instead of first calling you?

Every customer who does not contact you as regularly as they used to deserves a telephone call from you. Some important research must be done. Efforts must be extended to win back the customer. You already know that these referral sources or consumers have a need for your products or services. They also have some type of relationship with you, although it may be needing some repair. They may have had a bad experience with your company so you need to move quickly to ward off any bad press that they may be spreading about your business.

View the complaint as an opportunity.

By complaining, the professional or consumer gives you the opportunity to correct any problems that you may have caused. They are telling you they care about their relationship with your company and want to allow you the opportunity to correct a problem, and, hopefully, keep them as a customer. It may be difficult to view any complaint as positive; but you should see a complaint as a chance to fix a problem and win back the customer's esteem.

Fix the problem—not the blame.

Many employees take a complaint personally and become defensive. Stop deciding who is to blame and initiate a plan for fixing the problem. However, if you are in a managerial position, you may have to deal with an employee who has made a customer angry. This will take tact. Employees are usually very defensive when discussing their behavior. No one wants to be criticized for his actions.

You may want to begin your discussion by reminding the employee about the value of quality service. Acknowledge that it's easy to become stressed by customer problems, and that we may not be aware that others see us in a different light than we see ourselves. A private discussion with the individual who may be the source of the problems could save hundreds or even thousands of dollars in business. Make sure you are always discreet in repeating complaints or saying anything negative regarding the business practices of other employees.

Resolve problems quickly.

When a problem is brought to your attention, the sooner you are able to resolve it, the better it will be for the customer and your business. Problems should be noted immediately and brought to the attention of the appropriate person who can develop an action plan for solving the issue. When you hear about a problem that is causing one customer distress, you can make changes in your operation before other customers are affected. By taking quick action you may avoid losing other accounts.

Enhance your relationship with customers.

When dealing with a complaint, you may be afforded the opportunity to not only solve a problem, but to enhance your relationship with the customer. In the problem solution process you are afforded an opportunity to introduce and sell other products/services to the customer. You will definitely be put to the test. You will be given the opportunity to show how you can effectively handle a customer's stress. It may also be the opening for an important discussion about the customer's special needs or her demands for particular services or products. The complaint may have opened the door for you to learn more about the customer and for her to see a more personal side of you and your problem-solving skills. During a future staff meeting consider these thought-provoking questions.

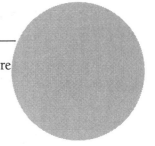

Value Received from a Complaint

1. Do you recall a customer who complained and with whom you now have a more positive relationship?

2. What did the customer complain about and what happened after he did?

3. Is there a customer who regularly complains but appreciates your patience and listening abilities?

4. Who is it and what do you do/say when you hear her complaints?

Provide a format for retaining information about complaints.

Knowing of problems and not doing nothing about them is a serious threat to an organization. You must begin by documenting problems so that they can be addressed in an organized manner. When the problems are recorded in writing it gives you a much better opportunity to think about and analyze occurrences, share incidents with other staff members, and make sure you have created an action plan for correcting the situation. Also, when you see more than one record with the same complaint, you know that you have a serious issue to deal with. If you see a trend happening, complaint after complaint all concerning the very same problem, you need to put up a red flag and intervene immediately to get the problem fixed.

Tracking problems through the use of a **complaint report** creates a permanent record of the complaint and the steps taken to address it. The record can also be a valuable tool to use in future training programs. The records should be periodically reviewed to again check the origins and causes of your complaints and to make sure the issues have been completely resolved to the customer's satisfaction. Figure 22.1 can be used as a guide if you wish to develop a complaint report for your organization.

Figure 22.1   Sample Copy of a Complaint Report

The Complaint Report

Person complaining _____ Company _____

Telephone _____ Fax _____ E-mail _____

Address _____

Complaining on behalf of _____ self _____ other patient/customer _____ family member

Date problem occurred _____ Persons/products involved _____

Date complaint received _____ How was it received? _____

What is the complaint about? In detail explain what the customer says is the complaint.

_____

What is the customer expecting from you? _____

Who originally told you about the complaint? _____

What did you tell or promise the customer in regards to handling the complaint? _____

_____

Who will be called to handle the complaint? _____

What will you do to handle the complaint? _____

When will you follow up to determine if the problem is solved? _____

Name of person taking the report of this complaint _____

Can you think of any other customer or employee who should be notified because of the complaint? _____

Who will you call? _____

Thank you for completing all the information in this report. This report is important for improving the services and products we provide. Your attention to these details is key to our continued efforts to improve customer service.

1. Why should you contact customers who haven't called in a long time?

_____

_____

_____

_____

2. In what way is a complaint an opportunity?

_____

_____

_____

_____

3. What should you say to an employee who has made a customer angry?

_____

_____

_____

_____

4. Why should you fix problems quickly?

_____

_____

_____

_____

5. Why should you document each complaint or keep a complaint record?

_____

_____

_____

_____

23

Comments to Avoid Saying to Customers

Objectives

- Identify comments that confuse customers.

- Understand how customers misinterpret remarks.

- Recognize and avoid statements that can create customer hostility.

When speaking to customers you may be unaware of exactly how you sound or how the message is interpreted. By carefully listening to what customers say you can discern what they appreciate hearing and what topics you should avoid. Experience becomes your best teacher with regard to understanding what dialogue is appropriate and pleasing to customers.

Certain comments and expressions are definitely off-limits. Listed and described in the sections that follow are a series of statements that may seem harmless. But when you choose certain words to put off offering your customer appropriate assistance, you create misunderstandings, even anger, and you fail to resolve the customer's problems. Worse yet, ill-chosen words may precipitate more problems. Review these expressions and see why they could be cause for alarm.

"I'll do the best I can."

What you are saying is that you haven't done the best you could up to now, but you will start. Most of your accounts thought you were doing your best and never suspected you would be giving anything less than 100 percent. They may now have proof that their initial feelings about how well you *were* going to perform was incorrect and that only *now* can they expect the very best!

"I don't know."

Frequently customers will make a request of someone in the office about a billing problem or service issue and the response they receive is "I don't know." While you may not know the answer to their questions, it is important to follow up with "But I will find out." Never end your part of the discussion without providing the information that the customer is requesting or giving them a time by which you will return with the information. Make sure you always offer to help the customer locate the answer.

"That's the second time I have heard that."

If you hear about a problem happening for the second time, *do not share* this information with the customer. No one wants to know that you knew about a problem, failed to solve it, and then allowed it to happen again, especially *to him*. Most customers think that once you have heard about a problem you would have developed a solution or decided not to provide a service or product that has given previous customers problems. Do not discuss the frequency of any of your problems with any customers.

"It's not my department."

This statement means you are passing the problem on to someone else. If at all possible, try to handle the situation quickly, or locate the person who is responsible for solving the problem. Refrain from telling the customer that it is not your department.

"I'll look into it."

The customer does not want the problem looked into—she wants it fixed. From the customer's perspective, she has already researched the issue and has determined that there is a problem. What she is now looking for is solutions. Your checking it out is not enough, nor does it appease her.

"The computer is down."

Does a computer that is not working mean you are closed? This seems to be the new excuse for not immediately taking the request for a product or service. Many companies act is if they are now incapable of writing up the order. Too often the consumer or nurse on the telephone is asked to call back later when the file they are referring to can be accessed and reviewed.

Try to avoid asking the customer to call back, because he may not. Take the order in the old-fashioned way—with paper and pencil, and later enter the information into the computer. Also, if you must speak with the customer again, *you* make the next call! While we all are becoming computer addicted, we must, when necessary, continue to do business manually. Paper and pencil can continue to generate business—even in today's high technology world. Do not let computer systems that are down affect your profits.

"That's not our policy."

Customers are not interested in your company policies. Many feel that their business is important enough for you to have a policy manual written just for them. They want to believe that they are an exception to any policy you have written. Be ready with explanations for the customer about why you cannot do something, without quoting them one of the policies from your manual. If it happens to be a policy from the federal government, you may want be ready to forward them a copy of the guidelines so they can more fully understand the rules that govern your industry and their request. It would be best to let them know this is not *your* policy but one generated by the government, and one that you are obliged to follow.

Office policies should be treated in a different manner. They were written with the customer in mind and to help manage an effective and profitable business. Do not let them prevent you from providing the best customer service. Policies should not make it more difficult to do what is best for both the business and the customer. Customers certainly do not want to hear about your policies as an excuse.

Policies should be reviewed and rewritten on a yearly basis, if not more often. Frequent complaints should cause you to examine policies and procedures immediately. Place their review dates on your calendar and analyze all of them before a crisis happens. After you receive a complaint you may want to consider evaluating the policy for appropriateness and accuracy, and for its ability to generate good business and customer satisfaction. It may be doing just the opposite.

Policies Needing Revision

Can you describe three company policies that may be preventing the delivery of quality service?

1. _____

2. _____

3. _____

"You should have told me that first."

The customer does not know what to tell you first. When taking the call, request, or order, if you are more concerned about where the customer lives or where the case manager works than any other concern, then you should be asking for that information first. The customer does not know in what order you would like to receive the information or what is most important to you. You need to guide the conversation. You must first ask for the information that will be the initial determining factor about whether you will even consider taking their business. You need to know what will determine your ability to meet the needs of the referral source or patient.

What I Need to Know First

What information do you need to know during your initial conversation with the customer?

1. _____

2. _____

3. _____

_____

"I have never heard of that happening."

If the customer tells you about a problem that has happened regarding a service or product that they have purchased from you, and you have never heard of that happening before, do not question the reality of the situation. We are not talking about *reality;* we are talking about *perception.* In the eyes and mind of the customer, it actually happened!

While it may be the first time you have heard such a story, do not discredit the comments made by the customer. Giving the appearance that you deny the validity of what the customer is saying will only create a hostile situation—something you certainly want to avoid. Here are some additional comments to avoid saying. Imagine how these remarks could create a storm of anger with your customers:

"You're crazy!"

"You really don't believe that, do you?"

"You sure are getting angry?"

"Calm down!"

"You have it all wrong."

"Don't you understand anything?"

1. How will your customer interpret the expression "I'll do the best I can"?
   _____
   _____
   _____
   _____

2. Should you let your customer know that her problem has happened before? Why not?
   _____
   _____
   _____
   _____

3. How can you handle a customer who wants to place an order when the computer is down?
   _____
   _____
   _____
   _____

4. How often should you review policies that affect customer service?
   _____
   _____
   _____
   _____

5. If a customer's problem is unique, does this mean it may not have happened?
   _____
   _____
   _____
   _____

24

Solutions to Customer Complaints

Objectives

- Develop effective approaches to problem solving.

- Learn to verify information.

- Understand the value of courtesy.

Once you've set up an effective system for identifying problems, you are ready to develop strategies for solving them. It would be a disservice to you and the organization to pinpoint what has gone wrong and then to do nothing to remedy the situation. Below are some practical guidelines to get your problem-solving operation off to a good start.

Learn to listen.

You must learn to listen carefully, since you cannot solve a problem unless you know all the details. Many of your customers could be overly stressed—busy professionals, anxious and upset patients, or family members frustrated in their new roles as caregivers—so their patience may be in short supply. You need to listen carefully and gather all the details regarding their complaint or request. Close your door, stop opening the mail, and pay full attention to the telephone call. Remember, don't take the complaint personally and refrain from becoming defensive.

Make sure that you have heard the entire problem.

It is very important to have all the details. You want to hear everything the customer is saying and understand completely what she is talking about. For this reason it is important that you request and verify all information given to you. Whatever went wrong once can happen again if you do not have all the correct information and understand what it means. You need accurate information to develop a plan of action that leads to an appropriate and correct solution.

Take time to repeat exactly what has happened and what is the problem.

Repeating the information provided by the customer will help you know exactly what the problem is before you begin solving it. You want to verify all the facts. You want this process to go smoothly since effectively and efficiently solving problems can enhance your image and really impress your customers. Take a moment to repeat the information you received. Recapping the scenario will help you and the customer reach agreement on what the problem is and what the goals for solving it will be.

Confirm that the caller has all the correct information (dates, times, telephone numbers).

Verify that the customer has all the correct information he needs or is requesting. You can repeat the information to him and then ask him to confirm that he has it right. Too often anxious customers or patients hear what they want to hear and miss many important details. Make sure they have all the important telephone numbers and account numbers that they require when and if they need to call you back. Because customers are often frustrated and confused by having to deal with a complex organization, it may help to mail them copies of the same information that you have provided on the telephone.

Ask the customer about other ways you can assist them.

While you may have solved one problem, others may be lurking in the background. It would be to your advantage to handle all of the problems now, before they grow in intensity and beyond their original importance.

Let the customer make some decisions.

Many of your customers are reluctant to be assertive and do not even know what they can be assertive about. If at all possible, allow them to make some decisions. The more power you impart to them in making decisions, the happier they will be. Can they decide the best time for the service to be delivered? Is the nurse or physician permitted to request how they want medical reports forwarded to their office? When selecting a product, are there any choices of color or size? Giving a patient a choice provides her with a degree of empowerment that may have been lost due to her medical condition. Everyone wants some control in an interaction. When the consumer asks if you can fax the report, he is expressing some control over the way he wishes to receive his information. At times it is best to relinquish some of your power and allow the customer more control.

Develop an action plan for solving problems.

Let the customer know what you are planning to do next. For example, when are you going to call her back with the information about the cost of her policy? When can she expect the delivery, or what report you will be sending her? Customers do not want to feel they have been forgotten or taken for granted especially when they are upset or concerned. Make sure they know what is about to happen in regards to your effort at providing quality service and solving their problems.

Show concern.

When the customer tells you about a problem, show sincerity and let him know you care about solving the crisis, saving the business relationship, and maintaining positive rapport. The customer must be made to feel that he is the most important element in your business. Express your concern about assisting him and in his receiving the service/ product in the manner that he had expected.

Thank the customer for calling.

While it may be personally difficult to thank the customer for complaining, it is this courtesy that often prevents the customer from calling the competition. Saying *thank you* has a strong positive influence. The customer has allowed you the opportunity to correct an unpleasant situation and save his business, so go for it. Show your gratitude and make it sincere.

Being warm and courteous helps cement long-lasting customer relations. When you make thanking customers a habit, people will continue to call your company. They will feel comfortable sharing their problems and concerns with you. They know you care about them and are dedicated to meeting their needs. When you are helpful and supportive, customers can open up, tell you what's bothering them, and put the problem in your hands. Courtesy and responsiveness to customer needs make good business sense.

Review Questions

1. Why is it important to hone your listening skills?

   _____
   _____
   _____
   _____

2. How can you verify that you have all the facts correct?

   _____
   _____
   _____
   _____

3. How can you empower the customer?

   _____
   _____
   _____
   _____

4. What do you accomplish by being warm and courteous?

   _____
   _____
   _____
   _____

25

Problem Solving Strategies

Objectives

- Understand the value of letting the customer assist in solving problems.

- Learn how to reach agreement with the customer.

- Outline the three stages for attacking a problem.

We are now ready to put the final touches on solving the customer's problems. Before we move any further, let's talk about the customer who is yelling at you. For example, there's the patient who cannot understand why the home care nurse is late for an appointment, or maybe it's a policyholder who's angry with a manager for not calling back as promised. When the customer is shouting at you, here are ways you can maintain control.

- Let them shout. It is impossible to speak with someone who is yelling at you.

- Speak in a lower tone of voice.

- Try to listen attentively so you can determine what is actually the problem.

- Continue to focus the conversation on what you can do to help, not on what you cannot do.

- Come to some agreement as to what is the *primary* problem and what you can agree should be done *first*.

- Restate the plan or the service that will now be provided.

- Acknowledge your understanding of the problems with words such as, "Yes, I do understand what you are referring to." In face-to-face encounters, use appropriate facial expressions.

How Do I Feel?

Briefly describe how you feel when a customer yells at you.

_____

What strategies do you use to manage their anger? _____

What are you thinking about as they are yelling? _____

_____

Do not take customers' anger personally. Because of stress many of your customers experience either at work or because of their illness, they project their frustration and you can become the target of their anger. While it is not easy to bear the brunt of unwarranted anger, you are not responsible for how badly they feel or how distressed they are. Being patient and calm under pressure is a job requirement. Once you have committed yourself to working with customers, you can predict that some displaced anger will be coming your way.

Suggest options for correcting problems.

All customers appreciate having options and choices. Usually you can take several approaches to solving the problem, and you should offer the customer as many alternatives as possible. While she may have her own suggestions for how she wants the situation addressed, you can present considerations that she may find accommodating.

Ask the customer about any suggestions she may have for solving the problem. Often the customer has some ideas that would meet her needs and are acceptable to you. Many times compromises can be easily made. The customer's solutions for solving the problem can often be incorporated into your plan of action.

Reach agreement with the customer regarding the best course of action.

Each problem to be solved must be mutually understood and agreed upon. If the solution has the approval of only _one_ party, it will not work. You must gain complete agreement from all concerned. Otherwise, the customer will have confused expectations and wind up not receiving what he wanted. Obtain agreement for your plan of action and then move ahead as quickly as possible toward resolution.

If the materials that the client requested have not reached his office and he is complaining about this, you will need to make another plan. You may agree to e-mail the documents, mail them again, fax, or forward them by a private mail service. A nurse who forgets to do something during the first visit may require you to schedule another visit later in the day. Whatever the new plan, make sure everyone agrees with the plan and has the same expectations regarding the outcome. In summary as you attack the problem:

1. *Understand* the entire problem. You cannot solve the patient/customer problem until you understand it and know all the facts.

2. *Identify* the cause of the problem and solicit suggestions from the customer that can be used for solving the problem. Through conversations with the customer, you will locate the source of the problem. This is important since the problem can very well happen again if you do not learn what caused it in the first place.

3. *Discuss and reach agreement* about the best course of action for solving the problem.

Exercise in Problem Solving

Identify a problem customers frequently have with your company.

What do you need to know about the problem before you can begin solving it?

What do you say or promise the customer after you have all the information?

When you have all the details, what are the next three steps to take?

1. _____

2. _____

3. _____

After the problem is solved, make sure you take time to discuss the case scenario with your colleagues and outline the approach you took to come to a resolution. The problem may occur again and you want to be prepared with one or more problem-solving strategies.

Review Questions

1. What are ways you can handle a customer who is angry and shouting?

   _____

   _____

   _____

   _____

2. How can you get the customer involved in problem solving?

   _____

   _____

   _____

   _____

3. Why should you ensure bilateral agreement to an action plan?

   _____

   _____

   _____

   _____

4. What are the three steps to finding a resolution?

   _____

   _____

   _____

   _____

Understanding Accreditation

Editor's Note:

Many professional bodies offer accreditation surveys to the health care community. In addition to the three accrediting bodies featured in this textbook, other organizations that are well known in the industry include:

- Accreditation Association for Ambulatory Health Care (AAAHC),
- Accreditation Commission for Health Care, Inc. (ACHC),
- CARF—The Rehabilitation Accreditation Commission,
- COLA (Commission on Office Laboratory Accreditation),
- Community Health Accreditation Program (CHAP), and
- International Organization for Standardization (ISO).

This section on accreditation is for educational purposes and should not be construed as an endorsement by HIAA or any of its member companies.

26

What Accreditation Is and What It Is Used For

Objectives

- Define how accreditation differs from licensing.

- Learn what accreditation means to consumers and employers.

- Understand why health care providers and health plans obtain accreditation.

Accreditation is a process whereby health care organizations voluntarily undergo a survey conducted by an independent outside entity that reviews operations, policies, documentation, and performance data to determine the degree to which the organization complies with the predetermined standards of practice used by the accrediting entity to evaluate health care organizations. Accreditation is similar to, but not identical with, licensure or certification. **Licensure** is granted by a government agency and is based on required compliance with a set of minimum prescribed criteria. Once a license is issued, the licensing agency focuses on finding deficiencies and enforcing regulations using citations and fines. Accreditation is voluntary, and its objective is to improve the performance of health care providers, health plans, or other health care organizations. An organization can earn various degrees of accreditation based on the level of compliance it achieves with specific standards. Both the process and the levels of accreditation will be discussed further in this chapter.

Accreditation standards are developed in consultation with health care experts, providers, measurement experts, purchasers, health care organizations such as HMOs and insurers, and consumers. When new standards are developed, experts from the particular area of health care delivery generally participate as subject matter experts. The standards are structured around a statement of intent which provides the rationale for the standard. The standards themselves are explicit goal statements that express the expectations that an organization must meet in order to achieve accreditation. For example, an accrediting agency might have a standard that addresses accessibility to care. The intent would be that providers are located within a reasonable distance of the membership they serve. The standard might state: "The organization has written standards to ensure the availability of providers based on the geographic distribution of its population." Compliance with the standard could be based on the percentage of the covered population that has at least two providers within a specified radius of home or work locations.

Accrediting bodies require organizations to have written policies and procedures that are consistent with the standards; they also look for evidence that the organizations are complying with the policies and procedures. They are not interested merely in what the organization is capable of, or says it can do, but rather in seeing demonstrable evidence of compliance with the policies and procedures used in daily operations. While it is acknowledged that standards themselves are not direct measures of quality, they are considered effective measures of predicting future performance.

Accreditation standards are updated periodically to improve clarity and address new information or technology. Occasionally new standards will be added to improve the quality of member care. For example, in recent years some accreditation organizations have developed prescribed service levels for behavioral health treatment. Some accreditation organizations circulate draft standards for public comment to assure broader input in the standards development process.

The three major health care accrediting organizations that this book will focus on are:

- **American Accreditation Healthcare Commission,** also known as **Utilization Review Accreditation Commission** (URAC). URAC is a private nonprofit organization founded in 1990 to establish standards for utilization review. URAC currently has 10 accreditation programs for the managed care industry.

- **Joint Commission of Accreditation of Healthcare Organizations** (JCAHO). JCAHO was founded in 1951 to act as a private independent accrediting body for hospitals. Since then, JCAHO has broadened its scope to include accrediting of entities delivering long term care, behavioral health care, laboratory, and ambulatory care services.

- **National Committee on Quality Assurance** (NCQA). NCQA is a private not-for-profit organization that includes accreditation surveys to assess the quality of HMOs and other managed care plans. In addition to accreditation, NCQA developed a set of data that measures key health care performance areas such as immunization and mammography screening rates. This **Health Plan Employer Data and Information Set** (HEDIS®) is an industry standard for outcomes and quality measurement. In addition to being a key component of accreditation surveys, HEDIS® is also used to compare the quality of health care outcomes across health plans regardless of whether a health plan chooses to undergo an accreditation survey.[1]

---

[1] See Appendix B for a listing of all URAC, JCAHO, and NCQA accreditations.

The Value of Accreditation

Most consumers are concerned about having their health care needs met. The average consumer is not educated about the benchmarks for measuring health care quality or what the various accreditations mean. Health plans hope to show consumers that by achieving accreditation they are earnest in their efforts to meet high standards and improve the quality of services provided.

Consumers who do even a little homework by looking at web sites will quickly see the benefit of selecting a health care organization that is accredited.

NCQA has a web site, www.healthchoices.com, which is designed to advise consumers on selecting a health plan. The site's main feature is the **Health Plan Report Card,** which provides comprehensive information about the NCQA accreditation status and the overall quality of the nation's health care organizations. By going to NCQA's main site (*www.NCQA.org*) consumers and purchasers can get more detailed information on accreditation, including HEDIS® data and accreditation information. This information helps people select the best health plan for their needs.

JCAHO dedicates a section of its web site (*www.JCAHO.org*) to the general public. It provides guidelines for helping consumers select the following health care services:

- ambulatory care,
- assisted living,
- behavioral health care,
- home health care,
- hospitals,
- lab services, and
- long-term care.

In addition, the JCAHO web site has questions to ask providers regarding medications, test results, and surgery.

URAC's web site (*www.URAC.org*) allows consumers to search for accredited organizations by state or by name. It also has a list of URAC-approved health web sites that consumers can visit to obtain information on health care issues. Other useful information at this site includes a summary of URAC standards and the accreditation process.

Purchasers of health care, such as corporate HR departments, check an organization's accreditation status when making purchasing decisions for health care coverage for employees. Because of increasing costs, employers are finding it difficult to maintain the current level of benefit packages. They are concerned that the money they do spend on health care coverage be spent wisely and provide value to their employees. An organization that has achieved accreditation has demonstrated that it has the systems in place to focus on quality of care and member service. The better the care and service are, the more satisfied purchasers and consumers will be.

The Accreditation Process

There are several parts to the survey process, depending on the accreditation being sought and the accrediting organization. The process generally includes:

- documentation review,
- interviews,
- chart or record reviews, and
- office tours.

Documentation Review. All surveys include a documentation review. This may be done on site or off site, depending on the accrediting organization. Surveyors review the organization's policies and procedures to assess the level of compliance with the standards. They also look for evidence that the organization is following its policies. Evidence may include committee meeting minutes, operational reports, satisfaction survey results, or any other relevant documentation.

Interviews. The interview process addresses a broad range of topics and issues relevant to the care and services provided by the health care organization. Interviewers speak with clinical leadership and staff involved in customer service, quality of care, and other relevant standards, depending on the type of accreditation the entity is seeking. JCAHO interviews patients and/or family members regarding their perceptions of the services and care rendered. Patient/family interviews may address patient rights, patient and family education, patient care, continuity of care, patient satisfaction, and other issues. In addition, JCAHO also requires surveyed organizations to provide an opportunity for members of the public to meet with a JCAHO survey team during each full on-site survey. This opportunity, called a public information interview (PII), is available to patients and their families, patient advocates, organization personnel, and other individuals who have quality of care or patient safety information to share with the survey team. *Source: www.jcaho.org*

Chart or Record Reviews. During the record review the surveyors review a selection of charts and records to assess compliance with relevant policies and standards. URAC and NCQA review complaint and appeal files. All organizations review provider credentialing files to ensure that all providers meet the necessary practice criteria, and blinded patient files to assess how providers organize and maintain patient treatment records. JCAHO also reviews staff files to assess staff education, orientation, and training.

JCAHO surveyors perform a facility tour by walking through the facility as patients do, starting from the parking area or the entrance to the building. The goal is to acquaint the surveyor with the environment and patient flow, assess the staff's orientation and knowledge of their duties and responsibilities, and review security, confidentiality, and patient/family education. *Source: www.jcaho.org*

Preliminary Report. Once the interviews, chart reviews, documentation reviews and other site work are complete, surveyors evaluate an organization's compliance against all applicable standards for the accreditation program and the population served. The surveyors generate a preliminary report listing strengths and weaknesses for the organization. These are presented at a closing conference at which the surveyed organization has an opportunity to ask questions about anything that is unclear and to solicit recommended courses of action from the surveyors. If there are strong differences of opinion as to the interpretation of any standards, the surveyor notes these comments in the report. This report is sent to the accrediting agency's executive review committees for review, approval, and final decision. *Source: www.jcaho.org*

Surveyor Qualifications

All surveyors are highly qualified and experienced individuals. For example, some of JCAHO's requirements for surveyors include:

- at least five years of leadership experience in the type of organization being surveyed; and

- a strong educational background—most surveyors have a master's degree and many have a clinical degree.

Prior to performing any surveys, new surveyors attend training, followed by a mentorship period with experienced surveyors. Surveyors receive ongoing education through annual evaluations and training programs. *Source: www.jcaho.org*

While the levels of accreditation vary with each accrediting body, they can be loosely categorized as follows:

- **Full accreditation**—The organization is in substantial compliance with the standards and there are no significant deficiencies.

- **Conditional accreditation**—The organization is in partial compliance with standards with some deficiencies in significant areas. A partial re-survey is usually required to bring deficiencies up to standard.

- **Denial**—This indicates that there are areas in which the applicant organization is substantially non-compliant with accreditation standards.

The Value Accreditation Brings to Customer Service

The three accreditation organizations have differing views on customer service. URAC focuses on the utilization management functions performed, JCAHO looks at patient rights and values, and NCQA evaluates access to information.

URAC standards require a complaint or grievance process for both patients and providers regarding utilization decisions. The grievance process must contain at least two levels of review and offer an external review for utilization management decisions that are not resolved by internal procedures.

Since JCAHO is primarily focused on locations where care is rendered, such as hospitals and other facilities, its standards address issues such as respecting patient rights; safeguarding personal dignity; respecting patients' psychological, cultural, and spiritual values; and conducting business relationships with patients and the public in an ethical manner. The standards further state that if satisfaction surveys contain complaints, the entity must objectively investigate the issue and contact the patient to communicate its findings and/or resolution.

In 1998, NCQA worked with the Agency for Healthcare Research and Quality (AHRQ) and the **Consumer Assessment of Health Plans Study** (CAHPS) Consortium to create a comprehensive **member satisfaction survey.** The survey measures a broad spectrum of customer satisfaction topics within the health care industry. Included in the survey are three questions about ease of access to customer service:

- finding information in the health plan's written materials;

- getting information from the health plan's customer service line; and

- dealing with paperwork for the health plan.

According to NCQA's *healthchoices.com* web site, from 1998 to 2000 health plans showed a composite improvement of 13 points in customer satisfaction based on CAHPS survey responses. The following chart is an excerpt from the 2000 survey information.

Questions Asked	Percent of Members Responding		
	A big problem	A small problem	Not a problem
How much of a problem, if any, was it to find or understand information in the written materials?	9.2%	33.6%	57.1%
How much of a problem, if any, was it to get the help you needed when you called your health plan's customer service?	15.4%	26.7%	57.9%
How much of a problem, if any, did you have with paperwork for your health plan?	4.7%	9.8%	85.5%

A composite score based on this information reveals that for 66 percent of the consumers surveyed, customer service was not a problem.

The largest impact accreditation has had on improving customer satisfaction is in the development of complaint, appeals, and grievance processes that give members the right to air their complaints and provide a structure for both internal and external review. In addition, access to information and ease of communicating with health plans has improved.

The Value of Accreditation to Overall Delivery of Health Care

The overall impact of accreditation on health care delivery is difficult to measure. Not all health plans, programs, or facilities go through the accreditation process. Those that do take steps to improve quality in accordance with the standards. In other words, they tend to improve what is being monitored. Outcomes studies show that organizations that undergo accreditation have better clinical outcomes than those that don't. However, even those organizations that choose not to be accredited will at some point need to improve their outcomes and operations in order to stay competitive. Therefore, accreditation has a direct impact on those organizations that pursue it, and an indirect impact on all health care organizations.

NCQA states, "The more consumers and employers use our information to help make decisions, the more of an incentive it gives these organizations to focus on quality. Accreditation is essentially a means of harnessing market pressure to improve the health care system."

One of the better known examples is the alleged health plan "gags" placed on physicians regarding what they could or could not say to their patients about treatment options. All accrediting organizations prohibit "gag clauses" in their standards.

Examples of Standards Designed to Improve Overall Health Care

All accrediting organizations require a quality management program designed to improve both clinical and non-clinical services.

NCQA

Improvement in clinical services can be seen in the NCQA Health Plan Employer Data and Information Set (HEDIS®). HEDIS® is a tool used by more than 90 percent of America's health plans to evaluate performance on significant aspects of care. It was designed to help purchasers and consumers compare the clinical outcomes and performance of managed health care plans. There are over 60 different HEDIS® measures.

Some of the areas HEDIS® measures include:

- asthma medication use,
- controlling high blood pressure,
- antidepressant medication management,

- advising smokers to quit,

- breast cancer screening, and

- childhood and adolescent immunization status.

Source: www.healthchoices.com

HEDIS® data are the main component of most health plan "report cards" that appear in national magazines and local newspapers. HEDIS® and CAHPS® provide the foundation data on which NCQA's **State of Managed Care Quality Report** is based. This report is an annual assessment and interpretation of key trends in the managed care industry. The data presented in this report are collected from health plans covering more than 63 million lives.

Consistent with the theory that what is observed and measured will improve, and what is not, will not, almost all areas covered on the HEDIS® and CAHPS® surveys showed improvement. The most impressive improvement was in the areas new to the surveys, specifically the control of cholesterol (+8.2 points) and blood pressure (12.5 points). The highest gains in member satisfaction were in claims processing (+3 points) and customer service (+2.1 points). In another promising measure, 59.3 percent of respondents rated their health plans as an 8, 9, or 10 on a scale of 1-10, a three-point increase over the prior year. A copy of the report can be downloaded from *www.ncqa.org*.

The **CAHPS® questionnaire** provides feedback on health plan performance in the area of customer satisfaction. There are 46 core questions, with the opportunity to add more based on the specialty services provided. The core questions measure member satisfaction in the following areas:

- claims processing,

- courteous and helpful office staff,

- customer service,

- getting care quickly,

- getting needed care, and

- how well doctors communicate.

Overall customer satisfaction is measured through the following:

- rating of all health care,

- rating of health plan,

- rating of personal doctor, and

- rating of specialist seen most often.

Source: www.healthchoices.com

NCQA's focus on managed care plans is grouped into five categories for improving care:

- Staying healthy—Does the health plan help people maintain good health and avoid illness? Is a full spectrum of preventive care (screenings, check-ups) covered? Does the plan have proactive immunization programs?

- Getting better—How well does the plan care for people when they become sick?

- Living with illness—How well does the health plan help people manage chronic illness?

- Qualified providers—Does the health plan thoroughly check the credentials of all of its providers?

- Access and service—Do health plan members have access to the care and service they need? Does the health plan resolve grievances quickly and fairly? How quickly can members get appointments?

Source: www.ncqa.org/aboutaccred.asp

JCAHO

The areas of care that JCAHO focuses on improving are:

- quality of care—how well the facility or practice determines the kind of care required to meet a patient's needs, both initially and as they change in response to care;

- qualified and competent staff—how the facility or practice addresses staff development, training, and competence;

- patient safety—how well an organization plans for necessary space, utilizes equipment and resources, and manages a safe environment;

- responsible leadership—how active a role the organization's leadership plays in planning, designing, and directing services; providing adequate staff and determining qualifications and competence; managing information; and improving performance.

- improving care and improving health—how well the organization monitors and analyzes patient outcomes to improve performance.

Source: www.jcaho.org

URAC

URAC measures performance against established standards in the following areas when accrediting health plans:

- scope of services—includes access to care, provider availability, and provider selection;

- health plan personnel—procedures for staff orientation and training;

- health plan operations—the integration of administrative and clinical operations, provider relations, provider credentialing, utilization management, and member relations;

- quality improvement—includes oversight of the program, improving clinical and nonclinical services;

- delegation of responsibilities—oversight of delegated responsibilities;

- confidentiality—processes and procedures for protecting member information; and

- grievance and complaint processes and procedures for both members and providers.

Source: www.urac.org

Organizations that undergo accreditation are able to demonstrate significant improvement in overall health plan quality from year to year. This is visible in operations, clinical outcomes, and customer service.

Why Insurance Companies, HMOs, Hospitals, Physicians, and Other Health Care Providers Obtain Accreditation

Health care providers and health plans go through the accreditation process to gain the competitive, operational, and regulatory benefits that come with accreditation. Rising premiums have turned the spotlight on the health care industry, and the political climate has made quality care an operational, financial, and competitive imperative.

Competition. In today's rapidly changing environment, providers and health plans are facing many competitive pressures in the marketplace. It is increasingly important to demonstrate to consumers, purchasers, and regulatory agencies a commitment to standards related to safety and quality of care. One of the best ways to demonstrate this commitment is by getting accredited by an organization whose goal is improvement in the quality of care.

Health care consumers are becoming more educated. Even if they don't know exactly what accreditation means, they know that it is better to have it than not. An ambulatory surgery center that is JCHAO accredited helps the patient feel more at ease that systems are in place to provide the best care possible. Similarly, a managed care plan with NCQA or URAC accreditation is known to have a commitment to improving the quality of health care.

Employers have become savvier purchasers of health care in recent years. As costs have risen, purchasers have started to demand higher quality and more accountability from health plans and providers. Most government purchasers and many large commercial purchasers require that a health plan be accredited in order to bid on new business. In turn, many health plans will contract only with facilities and providers that are accredited. Even if they do contract with facilities that are not accredited, they generally show a preference for placing patients requiring case management in facilities that have demonstrated their commitment to patient safety and quality outcomes. This is not to say that purchasing decisions are no longer based on cost, but rather that purchasers are looking at accreditation as an indicator of quality in conjunction with cost in evaluating the overall suitability of the health plan for their needs.

Operational. The accreditation process is rigorous and demanding. It often inspires organizations to institute new processes, form new committees, and substantially re-write their health care delivery policies and procedures, leading to improved results in patient outcomes and customer satisfaction.

The survey itself provides an objective evaluation of the organization's performance. It is designed to be educational and objective, not punitive. During the survey process, the health care organization has an opportunity to interact with the surveyors, who are experts in their fields and have seen many examples of successful health plans and facilities. The survey provides an excellent opportunity for consultation and staff education on quality issues. This support occurs throughout the survey as the surveyors offer suggestions for strategies that may help the organization better meet the standards and improve patient safety and quality of care.

The report that accompanies each accreditation decision can also be a valuable educational resource and development tool in that it details those areas where an organization's performance must improve and includes recommendations for how to meet the standards and improve performance.

Financial and Regulatory. Accreditation by URAC, JCAHO or NCQA can be used to meet certain Medicare certification requirements and often fulfills many state licensure requirements. This lessens the burden on federal and state regulators and allows one accreditation survey to take the place of several licensing and certification surveys. Additionally, many liability insurers consider accreditation as part of a risk management program, often leading to preferential premium rates on professional liability insurance.

Review Questions

1. How is accreditation different from licensing?

   _____
   _____
   _____
   _____

2. Why would consumers care if an organization is accredited?

   _____
   _____
   _____
   _____

3. Why would employers care if an organization is accredited?

   _____
   _____
   _____
   _____

4. What are three benefits to the organization being surveyed?

   _____
   _____
   _____
   _____

27

The Three Major Accrediting Bodies in Insurance and Managed Care

Objectives

- Understand the purpose and scope of the major accrediting bodies.

- Identify accrediting standards and survey processes.

- Learn how accrediting agencies define quality and improvement.

- Explore the steps in an accreditation survey.

Utilization Review Accreditation Commission (URAC)

Also known as American Accreditation Healthcare/Commission

History

URAC was founded in 1990 as a nonprofit organization to establish standards for the managed care industry. Many health plans, insurance companies, third party administrators (TPAs) and self-insured employers had embraced utilization review and management as effective methods for controlling health care costs but were concerned about the practices of some of the companies that had emerged to provide these services. The rumor mills generated such stories as: "a high school graduate was taking medical information and making decisions regarding lengths of hospital stays," "hospitals would not get return phone calls from medical management companies until the patient had already been discharged," and so on. Many felt the solution was the creation of uniform standards for those providing a variety of medical management services to the managed health and workers' compensation industries.

Organizational Structure

URAC has a small staff responsible for the day-to-day operations of its Washington, D.C. office. Staff members are assisted in their various tasks by volunteers from all sectors affected by managed care: employers, consumers, consultants, regulators, health care providers, health plans, insurance companies (health and workers' compensation), web site providers, and vendors.

These constituencies participate in the development and revision of the standards and are eligible to sit on the URAC Board of Directors. The Board of Directors is responsible for the final approval of all standards and accreditation of all organizations as well as policy development and strategy implementation for the organization.

What URAC Offers

URAC offers the following to the managed care and workers' compensation industries.

Accreditation Programs

Currently, there are 12 accreditation programs available for companies within the managed care industry:

- case management organizations,
- credential verification organizations,
- health call centers,
- health plan networks,
- health plans,
- health utilization management organizations,
- health provider credentialing organizations,
- workers' compensation networks,
- workers' compensation utilization management organizations,
- external review organizations,
- web sites of any managed care organization, and
- any managed care organization that wants to demonstrate to its stakeholders that it is committed to following core quality and customer service standards in its daily operations [Core Accreditation].

These programs have been developed by committees of experts (a committee for each set of standards) representing a diverse range of education, skills, and knowledge about the standards being developed. Experts in each particular area of health care delivery also participate in the development process, and URAC readily invites public comments on each set of standards as they are developed.

Generally, standards are updated every three years unless pressing legislative, regulatory, or industry events require updating on a more frequent basis.

The organization currently has additional accreditation programs under development which are scheduled to be released in 2002. These are for:

- claims processing organizations, and
- disease management companies.

Publications

URAC has published standards manuals that both interpret the standards and offer practical advice for developing and implementing policies and procedures that address the standards. URAC also offers a large number of other related publications. A visit to URAC's web site and publications link provides a list of these materials.

Educational Sessions and Conferences

URAC offers small, interactive workshops on its various accreditation programs in Washington, D.C. and around the country. Customized, on-site training is also available by contacting URAC directly.

Throughout the year, the organization also sponsors national conferences to introduce new standards and/or address issues that affect stakeholders and may impact current and future accreditation standards.

Research

To date, URAC's research activities have focused on workers' compensation performance measurement and preferred provider organization (PPO) performance measurement.

In 2001 URAC's focus was on researching how changes in the medical managed practices improve quality and accountability in the health care system.

The URAC Accreditation Process

URAC accredits many different types of managed care and workers' compensation companies. The critical factor in the accreditation process is not the type of company seeking accreditation but the functions it offers to its clients and customers.

Some of the accreditation programs focus on a single functional area while others focus on the organization as a whole. The process remains the same regardless of the areas being reviewed: A desktop review (done in the URAC offices in Washington, D.C.) focuses on the health care organization's policies and procedures as they relate to the accreditation being sought. An on-site visit to the company determines if the policies and procedures are being utilized in its daily operations.

A URAC staff member (lead reviewer) conducts the desktop and on-site reviews, often supported by additional staff reviewers. The lead reviewer presents the findings of both activities (desktop and on-site reviews) to the URAC Accreditation Committee.

The Accreditation Committee approves or disapproves the recommendation of the lead reviewer and sends it to the URAC Executive Committee for final approval.

All information presented to both committees is "blind" so that committee members are not aware of the company's identity.

This entire process (desktop review and on-site review) usually takes four to six months to complete once URAC receives the completed application packet.

If, after the desktop or on-site review, the lead reviewer feels that an organization is not ready for accreditation, URAC offers several options to assist the organization in choosing the best steps to take at that time. These steps range from consultative assistance to withdrawal of an application for consideration.

Accreditation costs vary by the type of accreditation. Typical fees paid to URAC include publication fees for copies of the accreditation standards the company is seeking, accreditation fee for the desktop and on-site reviews, and travel and out-of-pocket expenses related to the on-site visit.

Stakeholders and Customers

Many organizations have successfully sought and obtained accreditation from URAC. Reasons organizations undergo this process include:

- federal and/or state regulators require accreditation as a condition of doing business;

- clients require accreditation to consider an organization as a vendor; and

- the organization wants to demonstrate to its clients, prospective customers, and/ or regulators that it is a leader within its particular field(s) of expertise.

A complete list of companies accredited by URAC can be found on its website at *www.URAC.org.*

Joint Commission on Accreditation of Healthcare Organizations (JCAHO)

Organization

JCAHO has evaluated and accredited nearly 18,000 health care organizations and programs in the United States. JCAHO is a major participant in the accreditation of health care facilities such as hospitals, long term care facilities, home care agencies, ambulatory care organizations, and other related health care entities such as health maintenance organizations (HMOs), integrated delivery networks (IDNs), and preferred provider organizations (PPOs). Since its founding in 1951 as a private, not-for-profit organization, JCAHO has promoted the development of systems to better demonstrate quality of care, service, and delivery for facilities and provider networks providing health care services.

JCAHO is governed by a 28-member Board of Commissioners that includes nurses, physicians, consumers, medical directors, administrators, providers, employers, labor representatives, health plan leaders, quality experts, ethicists, health insurance administrators, and educators.

Scope of Accreditation Services

Over the past fifty years, JCAHO has developed accreditation programs for many clinical programs spanning the health care continuum. For a detailed listing of accreditation programs refer to *Appendix B: Accreditations Available by Accrediting Agency.*

In addition to the initial surveys and regular triennial survey, other types of surveys JCAHO conducts include:

- focused surveys,
- extension of accreditation surveys,
- random unannounced surveys,
- for-cause surveys,
- home health and hospice deemed status surveys, and
- corporate surveys.

Refer to *Appendix B: Accreditations Available by Accrediting Agency* for a detailed description of survey types.

In some states, the JCAHO survey process may substitute for federal certification for Medicare and Medicaid and/or fulfill federal and/or state licensure requirements.

Application for Accreditation Survey

Eligibility Requirements

The various JCAHO accreditation manuals listed in the Standards section below each contain extensive *Official Accreditation Policies and Procedures*. These list the general requirements for survey eligibility under the individual manuals (for example, *Comprehensive Accreditation Manual for Home Care* lists requirements for survey eligibility under the home care accreditation program). In addition, the policies and procedures contain provisions for survey options, information accuracy and truth, and disclosure of information to the public. *Accreditation Participation Requirements* are also detailed. In order for an organization to participate in the accreditation process, it must be deemed eligible for survey and comply with all *Accreditation Policies and Procedures* as well as *Accreditation Participation Requirements*.

Application

If an organization has never been previously surveyed, it contacts JCAHO and requests an application for an initial survey. The completed application provides JCAHO with information about the organization including ownership, scope of services, types of patients served, and volume and types of services provided. This information is used to determine the number of days needed for the survey and the staffing of the survey team. A JCAHO contact person is assigned to the organization to coordinate survey scheduling and serve as a resource.

Standards and Measurement

Performance Standards

JCAHO publishes manuals containing the standards for the various accreditation programs. These standards are reviewed and revised on an ongoing basis, with revised manuals published approximately every two years. The manuals currently include:

- Comprehensive Accreditation Manual for Ambulatory Care,
- Comprehensive Accreditation Manual for Behavioral Health Care,
- Comprehensive Accreditation Manual for Health Care Networks,
- Comprehensive Accreditation Manual for Home Care,
- Comprehensive Accreditation Manual for Hospitals,
- Comprehensive Accreditation Manual for Long Term Care (includes standards for dementia special care units and subacute care programs),
- Comprehensive Accreditation Manual for Pathology and Clinical Laboratory Services,
- Comprehensive Accreditation Manual for Preferred Provider Organizations,
- Comprehensive Accreditation Manual for Managed Behavioral Health Care, and
- Comprehensive Accreditation Manual for Assisted Living Communities.

Performance Measurement

In February 1997, JCAHO launched yet another initiative in its mission to continuously improve the safety and quality of care provided to the public through the accreditation process and related performance improvement activities. JCAHO's **ORYX®** initiative incorporates outcomes and other performance measurement data into the accreditation process. This allows JCAHO to review data trends and patterns and to work with organizations as they use data to improve the delivery of patient care services. By reviewing performance data submitted by organizations to JCAHO, the accreditation organization is better able to target areas for the regular accreditation survey, continuously monitor an accredited organization's performance, and support and stimulate the organization's continuous performance improvement efforts. In this manner, more of the survey process is driven by data rather than a potentially subjective review by surveyors.

The next step in the ORYX® performance measurement initiative is the identification and use of core measures. These are standardized performance measures that can be applied across accredited health care organizations for comparison purposes in a particular accreditation program. In the future, JCAHO anticipates using core measure data from an organization to assist in focusing the organization's on-site survey evaluation activities. (Note: Hospitals will be the first group to begin collecting core measure data for patient discharges beginning July 1, 2002. Other types of organizations will follow as additional core measure sets are identified by JCAHO.)

Scoring

Each chapter of the various accreditation manuals contains performance-based standards that focus not only on what the organization has in place (for example, committees, policies and procedures), but what it does with these structures. The activities carried out ultimately impact the safety and quality of care being delivered. On a five-point scale, the organization is scored by the surveyor for compliance with the standards and their intent statements. While it is expected that accredited organizations will maintain continuous compliance throughout the interval between surveys, for practical purposes the surveyors limit their review to the organization's track record of compliance for a period of one year before a triennial survey. During an initial or focused survey, the required track record for full compliance is generally the four months preceding the initiation of the survey.

Survey Process

To earn and maintain accreditation, most organizations must undergo an on-site survey by a JCAHO survey team at least once every three years. Laboratories must be surveyed every two years. The actual survey process is a combination of on-site activities described in Chapter 26 of this manual—documentation review, policy and procedure review, conferences with organizational leaders, and, most importantly, interviews with patients, families and staff members. JCAHO's survey process focuses more on the *performance* of the various functions within the organization rather than whether or not documents or committee minutes are in place.

Since implementing its *Agenda for Change* in 1986, JCAHO has moved from a survey process similar to that of certification or licensure to a more functional approach. The JCAHO survey focuses on the *performance* of an organization rather than its *ability* to perform. Performance relates to key organizational or patient care functions most important to achieving quality results. These key functions are composed of organizational processes and systems which are directly related to patient care or support patient care. These functions are the basis for the JCAHO standards manuals and comprise the actual chapters of the various manuals. Refer to *Appendix C: Overview by Accrediting Agency of the Major Standards Areas*.

With the further implementation of the ORYX® performance measurement initiative, organizations being surveyed are asked to explain:

- their rationale for the selection of performance measures;
- how ORYX® data have been analyzed and used for the improvement of organizational performance; and
- the results of these performance improvement activities.

As JCAHO raises the bar on performance measurement and requires that organizations collect and submit core measure data, surveyors will assess the health care organizations' use of selected core measure sets in their performance improvement activities.

Accreditation Decision

At the completion of the scheduled survey activity, the surveyors review their findings and, with the assistance of laptop-based, decision-support software, provide the organization's leadership with a preliminary report of findings.

Several weeks later, JCAHO provides the organization with an accreditation decision in its *Official Accreditation Decision Report* which may or may not contain changes from the preliminary report. There are six possible accreditation decisions.

- *Accreditation without Type 1 Recommendations*—The health care organization demonstrates satisfactory compliance with applicable JCAHO standards in all performance areas.

- *Accreditation with Type 1 Recommendations*—The health care organization demonstrates satisfactory compliance with applicable JCAHO standards in most performance areas but has deficiencies in one or more performance areas or accreditation policy requirements that require resolution within a specified time period.

- *Provisional Accreditation*—The health care organization has demonstrated satisfactory compliance with a subset of standards during a preliminary on-site evaluation. This decision category is then replaced with one of the other official accreditation decision categories at the time of complete survey with all applicable standards, approximately six months later. This accreditation decision applies only to organizations seeking initial accreditation.

- *Conditional Accreditation*—The organization fails to demonstrate satisfactory compliance with applicable JCAHO standards in multiple performance areas, is persistently unable or unwilling to demonstrate satisfactory compliance with one or more JCAHO standards, or has failed to comply with one or more specified accreditation policy requirements but is believed to be capable of achieving satisfactory standards compliance within a stipulated time frame.

- *Preliminary Denial of Accreditation*—There is justification to deny accreditation to a health care organization because the organization has failed to demonstrate satisfactory compliance with applicable JCAHO standards in multiple performance areas or accreditation policy requirements, or for other reasons. This accreditation decision is subject to subsequent review.

- *Accreditation Denied*—The health care organization has been denied accreditation. This decision becomes effective only when all available review and appeal opportunities have been exhausted or forfeited. This decision category remains in effect until the end of the organization's accreditation cycle or until the organization has a new survey prior to the end of this cycle that results in a different accreditation decision.

Source: Joint Commission on the Accreditation of Healthcare Organizations, 2001.

National Committee for Quality Assurance (NCQA)

Overview

NCQA is a private, not-for-profit organization dedicated to assessing and reporting on the quality of managed care plans. Its stated mission is to improve the quality of health care delivered to people everywhere. NCQA evaluates health care quality in three ways:

- accreditation, an on-site review of key clinical and administrative processes;

- the Health Plan Employer Data and Information Set (HEDIS®), a tool used to measure performance in key areas such as immunization and mammography screening rates; and

- a comprehensive member satisfaction survey (CAHPS 2.0).

The intention is to encourage health plans to compete on quality and value, rather than price and provider network. *Source: www.ncqa.org*

History

NCQA was established in 1990 and conducted its first accreditation survey in 1991. By 1996, almost half of the nation's HMOs were participating in NCQA accreditation surveys, and by 1998 almost 90 percent were collecting some HEDIS® data. Nearly 75 percent of Americans enrolled in an HMO are in a health plan that has been reviewed by NCQA.

In 1992, NCQA began to develop HEDIS® as a measurement tool. In 1995, it introduced a certification program for credentials verification organizations. In 1997, it launched accreditation for managed behavioral health care organizations (MBHOs) and a certification program for physician organizations. In 2001, NCQA accredited its first preferred provider organization (PPO). In the future, NCQA plans to evaluate medical groups and individual providers as well. *Source: www.ncqa.org*

Stakeholders

Stakeholders include consumers, employers providing health benefits, policy makers, organized medicine, insurers, and health plans.

- Consumers who are not savvy about the health care industry and the myriad of plans available can quickly assume that an accredited health plan has processes in place to ensure quality care. NCQA has a consumer-oriented web site, *www.healthchoices.com*, that explains the criteria used for accrediting health plans and lists accredited health plans by geographic area.

- Employers and other purchasers of health care use NCQA accreditation to assist them in making purchasing decisions. Accreditation can help to distinguish a health plan on something other than network and price.

- Policy makers are stakeholders in NCQA to the extent that they can reduce the amount of oversight and monitoring of plans that are accredited. In some instances, an NCQA accreditation will be deemed as meeting a government survey standard.

- In the just over 10 years that NCQA has been in existence, it has exerted a tremendous influence on health care practices. Many of the standards that health plans must meet in order to become accredited require cooperation and collaboration with health care providers. Thus, in order to enter into a contract with an NCQA accredited health plan, providers must comply with certain standards of practice and quality policies.

- Finally, the health plans themselves are the largest stakeholder. Many health plans spend considerable human and capital resources revising their operations, policies, procedures, and committee structures in order to achieve compliance with the standards and improve their HEDIS® and CAHPS results.

The Accreditation Process

Accreditation is a rigorous and comprehensive evaluation process through which NCQA assesses the quality of the key systems and processes that make up a health plan. In particular, NCQA evaluates health plans in the areas of patient safety, confidentiality, consumer protection, access, service, and continuous improvement. Accreditation also includes an assessment of the care and service that health plans are delivering in such key areas as immunization rates and mammography rates.

Accreditation goals and objectives are as follows:

- **Evaluate organizations based on results.** NCQA evaluates audited HEDIS® performance results and evaluates those results against thresholds and benchmarks. All accreditation outcomes are based on both audited HEDIS® results and performance to published standards.

- **Provide purchasers and consumers with better information.** The information included on a health plan report card makes health plan performance data easier to understand and use when selecting a plan based on quality results.

The Survey Process

At the health plan's request, NCQA sends a team of trained health care providers, physicians, and managed care experts to conduct a rigorous, on-site review of the health plan. The expert reviewers evaluate the plan's core systems and processes, combining information from the on-site review with information from health plan records and consumer surveys. NCQA conducts an on-site survey at least every three years depending on prior performance and other circumstances (lower accreditation scores necessitate a re-survey sooner than three years). Survey personnel consist of physician and administrative surveyors. Most site visits are between two and four days in duration. During the site visit NCQA reviews quality processes and assesses the extent to which the organization is in compliance with NCQA standards. On-site surveyors utilize the following techniques to assess compliance levels:

- review written documentation,

- review and score credentialing files,

- review and score medical records,

- review and score appeals files,

- review and score utilization management case files,

- review handling of complaints and appeals,

- review member survey results,

- conduct staff interviews, and

- observe the organization's operations.

Performance Criteria

Health plans undergoing accreditation are reviewed against more than 60 standards designed to evaluate the health plan's clinical and administrative systems. Compliance with standards accounts for 72.5 percent of the points. The standards and measures fall into five broad categories:

- **Access and Service.** Do health plan members have access to the care service they need? For example: Do patients report problems getting needed care? How well does the health plan follow up on grievances? To evaluate these activities, NCQA reviews appeals and health plan denial records, interviews health plan staff, and grades the results from consumer surveys.

- **Qualified Providers.** Does the health plan assess each doctor's qualifications and what health plan members say about the providers? For example: Does the health plan regularly check the licenses and training of physicians? Does the health plan check whether physicians have had sanctions or lawsuits brought against them? How do health plan members rate their personal doctors or nurses? To evaluate these activities, NCQA uses records of doctors' credentials, interviews health plan staff, and grades the results from consumer surveys.

- **Staying Healthy.** Does the health plan help people maintain good health and avoid illness? Do children receive all appropriate immunizations? Do women receive mammograms as recommended? NCQA evaluates health plan activities that help people maintain good health and avoid illness. For example: Does the health plan give its doctors guidelines on how to provide appropriate preventive health services? Are members receiving tests and screenings as appropriate? To evaluate these activities, NCQA reviews health plan records, grades independently verified clinical data, and reviews materials sent to members.

- **Getting Better.** How well does the health plan care for people when they become sick? How does the health plan evaluate new medical procedures, drugs, and devices to ensure that patients have access to safe and effective care? Do doctors in the health plan advise smokers to quit? To evaluate these activities, NCQA reviews health plan records and interviews health plan staff.

- **Living with Illness.** How well does the health plan care for people with chronic conditions? Do diabetics, who are at risk for blindness, receive eye exams as needed? Does the plan have programs in place to assist patients in managing chronic conditions like asthma?

Source: www.ncqa.org

Scoring

In addition to the on-site survey, health plans must report on their clinical performance using HEDIS®. HEDIS® results account for 27.5 percent of the possible 100 points. Of the 22 measures that are evaluated, 12 are HEDIS® clinical measures and 10 are HEDIS®/CAHPS 2.0 results. The HEDIS®/CAHPS 2.0 results measure consumer experience. For the HEDIS® results, NCQA assigns points for each measure depending on where the results fall compared with regional and national benchmarks. A health plan can earn up to 15 points for the HEDIS® clinical measures and 12.5 points for the HEDIS®/CAHPS 2.0 results.

Accreditation

NCQA offers five possible accreditation levels.

- *Excellence*—The highest accreditation outcome is granted only to those plans that demonstrate a level of service and clinical quality that meet or exceed NCQA's requirements for consumer protection and quality improvement. Plans earning this accreditation level must also achieve HEDIS® results that are in the 90th percentile of national or regional performance.

- *Commendable*—This outcome is awarded to plans that demonstrate levels of service and clinical quality that meet or exceed NCQA's requirements for consumer protection and quality improvement.

- *Accredited*—Health plans that earn the accredited outcome must meet most of NCQA's basic requirements for consumer protection and quality improvement.

- *Provisional*—This level of accreditation indicates that a health plan's service and clinical quality meet some, but not all, of NCQA's basic requirements for consumer protection and quality improvement. NCQA does not issue an accreditation seal for the provisional status.

- *Denied*—Denied is an indication that a health plan did not meet NCQA's requirements during its review. NCQA does not issue an accreditation seal for the denied status.

Source: www.ncqa.org

The NCQA Quality Cycle

A key component in the accreditation process is the demonstration of performance and, upon re-accreditation, meaningful improvement in both clinical and service areas. For clinical areas, HEDIS® measures usually point out areas in need of improvement. In service areas, the CAHPS 2.0 measures show improvement opportunities. In order for an improvement to be meaningful, it must be relevant to the population and be likely to result in better outcomes. An improvement needs to be attributable to the health plan's actions and not one that happened by chance. Additionally, it should have an impact on high-volume, high-risk or high-cost conditions or services. For example, improvements in outcomes that impact 50 percent of the population are considered more meaningful than improvements that impact one percent of the population. The improvement must be associated with an appropriate study design and include:

- a clear rationale with objectives that are relevant to the target population;

- a clear statement of purpose that ensures that the method used to gather data is consistent with the rationale and target population;

- appropriate measures and data analysis; and

- strong and targeted actions.

Consistent with demonstrating overall improvement in clinical and service measures resulting from the quality improvement program, standards focus on providing appropriate levels of care and service to members. To this end many standards require the health plan to:

- establish standards regarding quality performance (for example, establishing timeliness standards for responding to appeals);

- collect and analyze data to measure performance against the standard;

- identify opportunities for improvement and decide which opportunities to pursue;

- implement interventions to improve performance; and

- measure effectiveness of interventions.

By following these quality initiatives health plans can make significant strides in attaining accreditation.

Review Questions

1. What brought about the need for accreditation of managed care companies in the early 1990s?

   _____

   _____

   _____

   _____

2. How long does it typically take for a company to be accredited by URAC?

   _____

   _____

   _____

   _____

3. How often are URAC standards revised?

   _____

   _____

   _____

   _____

4. In addition to receiving accreditation, what other licensure/certification benefits might an organization receive from the survey process?

   _____

   _____

   _____

   _____

5. What is the major focus of a JCAHO survey?

   _____

   _____

   _____

   _____

6. How often does an organization have to go through a JCAHO survey in order to maintain accreditation?

   _____

   _____

   _____

   _____

7. List three NCQA stakeholders.

_____

_____

_____

_____

8. Name the techniques that NCQA uses during an on-site survey.

_____

_____

_____

_____

9. What are the five categories that comprise NCQA standards?

_____

_____

_____

_____

10. How does NCQA define meaningful improvement?

_____

_____

_____

_____

28

Accreditation Standards That Relate to Customer Service

Objectives

- Understand core standards that pertain to patients.

- Know the difference between a complaint and an appeal.

- Learn how member satisfaction is measured.

- Describe what accessibility and availability mean.

- Identify data that accrediting agencies collect to ensure customer/ patient service issues are being addressed.

Accreditation standards cross a wide spectrum covering many aspects of health care delivery. This chapter addresses those standards that relate specifically to customer service.

URAC Core Standards of Quality

URAC has many accreditations available for managed care organizations. One of these is titled **Core Standards for Organizational Quality.** These core standards are "designed to apply to any organization in the planning, management, and administration of health care services" and are also incorporated into the standards for each accreditation available.

The Core Standards of Quality, which relate to interactions with customers, patients, insureds, and enrollees, are the following:

1. The organization must maintain written policies and procedures that govern all aspects of its programs. All policies and procedures are reviewed annually and revised as necessary.

   Customer service impact: Ensures that all customers will receive the same treatment for each situation. Also provides the "answers/responses" to enable frontline staff to handle situations as they arise, thus putting the customer first.

2. The organization has established and implemented mechanisms to promote coordination and communication across departments and disciplines within the organization. The emphasis is to ensure integration of administrative activities, clinical operations and quality improvement.

   Customer service impact: These mechanisms allow customers to avoid the traditional "runaround" that can occur when one department hands off an issue to another department without passing on relevant information, thus forcing the customer to start from the beginning in order to receive resolution and satisfaction.

3. The organization has written job descriptions for each position, and each staff member must meet each item in the description including qualifications, professional competencies, appropriate licensure/certification (where required) and scope of roles and responsibilities. Staff must receive initial training before carrying out responsibilities and have access to ongoing training as necessary to maintain professional competency.

   Customer service impact: Customers will receive services from staff possessing the necessary skills, knowledge, and education, as well as customized training in the company's policies and procedures. This allows customers to receive the appropriate level of service from a staff person on the appropriate level.

4. The organization has a well-defined organizational structure outlining the direct and indirect responsibilities for all clinical and operational functions and departments within the organization.

   Customer service impact: Appropriate levels of supervision and management are available to handle customer service issues as they arise. Additionally, customers can be told who is responsible for a particular problem and are able to access that person directly if additional assistance is needed following communication with frontline staff.

5. The organization has a communications plan to inform consumers of their rights and responsibilities; further, it follows marketing procedures that clearly and accurately communicate information about the organization's services to the customer.

   Customer service impact: Customers know what they can expect from the organization and what they are expected to do in the business relationship.

6. The organization has a method(s) to collect information about consumer satisfaction and utilizes the method(s) on a regular basis.

   Customer service impact: Feedback from customers forms the basis of good customer service. By getting input from customers, organizations can improve products and services and create new ones needed by customers.

7. The organization has internal standards to ensure service levels, often called **performance benchmarks.** The organization has procedures in place to monitor performance against the benchmarks and a process to improve customer service when the benchmarks are not met.

Customer service impact: Customers are guaranteed that the organization is committed to providing services to its customers, and there are written descriptions as to when, how, and where these services must be performed.

8. The organization has a system in place to receive and respond to consumer complaints as well as a grievance process that allows customers to take additional steps if they are not satisfied with the initial response to their complaint. The initial decision by the organization must be provided to the customer in writing and include: 1) the final determination; 2) an explanation of the reason for the determination; and 3) information on how the customer may seek further review.

Customer service impact: Provides customers with a formal method of ensuring action on their complaints and/or grievances, and informs them of additional avenues to pursue if they are not satisfied with the initial decision.

9. The organization has a written quality management program in place and being implemented throughout all areas and functions within the organization. The purpose of the program is to promote objective and systematic monitoring and evaluation of customer service and health care services. The monitoring of results and corrective action steps when the quality standards are not met is to be done by a quality management committee. This committee has the authority and responsibility for the oversight of the plan and reports directly to the organization's governing body.

Customer service impact: The governing body of the organization has an active committee whose sole purpose is to monitor and review the performance of the organization as it relates to clinical and administrative services provided to customers. This committee serves as a "consumer watch dog" at a very responsible level within the organization.

Source: www.urac.org

JCAHO Rights and Ethics Standards

The JCAHO accreditation standards specifically relating to customer/patient/insured/ enrollee service are primarily addressed under the standards chapters for Rights and Ethics located in each of the 10 JCAHO standards manuals. The evaluation of the effectiveness of this patient service function is addressed in the Improving Organizational Performance standards. While the numbering of the various standards may differ in the various manuals, the core content is the same and is outlined below in the JCAHO standards.

Patient Rights

The goal of the rights and ethics function is to "help improve patient outcomes by recognizing and respecting each patient's rights during the provision of care or services and conducting business relationships with patients and the public in an ethical manner." (JCAHO, 2001). It is the intention of these standards to ensure that care and services are provided in such a way as to respect and foster in individuals served a sense of dignity, autonomy, positive self-regard, civil rights, and involvement in the provision of their own care and services. The standards relating to patient rights are as follows:

1. The organization must affirm the patient's right to make decisions regarding his or her care. Further, the organization helps the patient exercise his or her rights by:

   • providing the patient with a written statement of the organization's mission and the scope of care or services provided to the patient directly or through contractual arrangement;

   • providing the patient with the hours during which care or services are available and how the patient can obtain care or services after hours, as applicable;

   • ensuring that patient rights are an integral part of all policies and procedures related to care or services provided by the organization;

   • being considerate of the patient's personal, cultural, and ethnic preferences; and

   • ensuring that all staff understand and respect patient rights, and provide care or services that reflect this understanding.

   Customer service impact: Patients understand that they have rights and that their rights are acknowledged and respected.

2. The patient is informed of his or her rights in a manner which he or she understands.

   Customer service impact: Patients are informed of their rights at admission (first visit) and on an ongoing basis, as necessary. This information is provided to patients in writing and in a manner in which they understand.

3. Provisions must be made for the patient to participate in decisions regarding his or her care or services whenever possible and to the extent of his or her cognitive abilities. The patient receives clear and concise explanations from staff members who are knowledgeable about:

   • the patient's condition;

   • the nature and purpose of any proposed care or service(s);

   • the potential benefits, risks, and effects of the care or services, their likelihood of success, and potential problems;

   • who will perform the care or services; and

   • the actual dollar amount in writing, if any care or services are to be borne by the individual.

   Further, the patient's right to make informed decisions regarding proposed or ongoing care or services extends to the following:

   • resolution of any conflicts or ethical issues which may arise;

   • the right to decide to discontinue care or services or refuse part or all of care or services to the extent permitted by law (The organization must inform the patient of the expected consequences of the refusal of care or services.); and

   • the right for the patient's family or guardian to exercise the patient's rights when the patient has been judged incompetent.

Customer service impact: The patient has a right to make informed decisions regarding proposed and ongoing care or services.

4. The patient or the patient's legal guardian must give informed consent prior to participating in research, investigational or experimental studies, or clinical trials.

   Customer service impact: The patient has the right to choose whether or not to participate in research, investigational or experimental studies, or clinical trials.

5. Staff should communicate with the patient in a language or form understandable to the patient taking into consideration communication barriers related to expressive aphasia, deafness, blindness, non-English speaking and/or limited education.

   Customer service impact: The patient has the right to have communication needs met.

6. Patients are free to voice complaints regarding policies, care, or services and to recommend changes without being subject to coercion, discrimination, reprisal, or unreasonable interruption of care or services.

   • At admission or first visit, the organization informs the patient of the complaint resolution process and other resources for registering complaints.

   • The organization investigates and responds to complaints and recommendations received from patients.

   Customer service impact: The patient has the right to have complaints heard, reviewed, and, if possible, resolved.

7. The organization respects and protects the confidentiality of all information concerning patient care or services. Protecting the patient's right to confidentiality includes both written and verbal communication of such information.

   Customer service impact: The patient has a right to confidentiality of information.

8. The organization respects the patient's personal and environmental privacy and security. Privacy and security include:

   • visual and auditory privacy during personal care or examinations;

   • respect for the patient's property during visits, hospitalizations, etc.; and

   • reasonable steps are taken to ensure that the patient's security is not compromised while visiting health care organizations or receiving home visits.

   Customer service impact: The patient has a right to privacy and security.

9. The patient has the right to formulate advance directives. The patient has the right to appropriate assessment and management of pain. (These are clinically related patient rights standards.)

   Customer service impact: The patient has the right to be involved in the planning of his or her care.

Organization Ethics

1. The organization must identify ethical issues and issues prone to conflicts and develop a process to handle issues when they arise. It must educate staff about available alternatives, ethical aspects of care or services, and processes to address ethical issues.

   Customer service impact: The organization addresses ethical issues in patient care or services.

2. The organization's policies and procedures regarding admission, transfer, referral, discharge, and billing practices support legal and ethical business practices. The organization must also inform the patient of any financial benefit received by the referring organization when he or she is referred to another organization for care or services.

   Customer service impact: The organization conducts its business ethically within the scope of law and regulation and in the best interests of the patients it serves.

3. The organization's governing body must review the organization's relationships with other health care providers, education institutions, and payers to ensure that these relationships are within law and regulation.

   Customer service impact: The organization addresses ethical issues in the relationship of the organization, its staff, and its governing body with other health care providers, educational institutions, and payers.

4. Clinical decisions must be based on identified patient health care needs rather than compensation or financial risk shared with leaders, managers, clinical staff, and physicians. Policies and procedures and information about financial incentives must be available to the surveyor upon request.

   Customer service impact: When the organization provides financial incentives to its staff, the organization must have a process to ensure that the integrity of clinical decision making is not compromised.

Improving Organizational Performance

Data Collection

JCAHO requires that data be collected on the needs, expectations, and satisfaction of individuals and organizations served. This requirement is based on the understanding that information gathered from patients and family members can provide insight about process design and functioning. The organization can use a number of ways to receive input including satisfaction surveys, regularly scheduled meetings with patient groups, and focus groups.

Public Information Interview

JCAHO further stresses the importance of customer service and client/staff satisfaction by including the public information interview as part of the survey process. The purpose of the interview is to obtain information about the organization's compliance with accreditation standards by interviewing all individuals—including patients and families, physicians, referral sources, employees, and residents from the community at large—who request an opportunity to speak with a surveyor. If the interviewee's statement involves complaints or problems that can be substantiated during the actual on-site survey, the surveyor has the option of including these issues as recommendations for improvement in the accreditation report.

In its Accreditation Policies and Procedures, JCAHO dictates the procedure for public information interview notification to its patients, staff, and the community. Failure to comply with these procedures may result in a Type 1 recommendation, which in turn may jeopardize the accreditation status of the organization.

Public Information Policy

In addition to assisting organizations in improving their performance through the accreditation process, JCAHO is committed to making performance information about health care organizations available to consumers and purchasers in order for them to make informed choices when selecting health care providers. This is accomplished by accessing the JCAHO Performance Report, which is available in hard copy from JCAHO or through the JCAHO web site at *www.jcaho.org*. The performance report provides summary information about an organization's performance during the accreditation survey process and compares this data with other similar organizations surveyed. It is anticipated that future performance reports will also include performance measurement data of organizations accredited by JCAHO. (Refer to JCAHO Official Accreditation Policies and Procedures for detailed listing of contents of performance reports.)

Sources:

- *Joint Commission on the Accreditation of Healthcare Organizations, (2001), Standards Manual for Home Health, Personal Care, Support Services 2001-2002.*

- *Joint Commission on the Accreditation of Healthcare Organizations, (1998), Understanding Your Rights in Managed Care Health Plans.*

NCQA's Customer Service Standards

NCQA's customer service standards are addressed in the quality improvement, utilization management and members' rights and responsibilities sections. Here, the customer is defined as the subscriber and member seeking treatment. There are additional standards that address provider satisfaction; however, those standards are not documented here. The following standards are taken from the NCQA MCO Surveyor Guidelines.

Quality Improvement

Quality improvement standards are concerned with the availability of and accessibility to primary care physicians, specialty physicians, and behavioral health practitioners. Quality improvement standards also address member satisfaction.

Availability

Availability means there is a sufficient number of providers in the network to serve the needs of the membership. It also takes into account the cultural, linguistic, and gender preferences of members. Following is a sampling of NCQA standards for availability.

- The managed care organization ensures that its network is sufficient in numbers and types of practitioners.
- In creating and maintaining its delivery system of practitioners, the managed care organization takes into consideration assessed special and cultural needs and preferences.
- The managed care organization implements mechanisms designed to ensure the availability of primary care practitioners.
- The managed care organization implements mechanisms designed to ensure the availability of specialty care practitioners.

Accessibility

Accessibility standards are concerned with the ability of the membership to access member service, behavioral health providers, and other practitioners on a timely basis. Below is a sampling of NCQA standards for accessibility.

- The managed care organization establishes mechanisms to assure the accessibility of primary care services, behavioral health services and member services.
- The managed care organization establishes standards for access to medical care.
- The managed care organization establishes standards for key elements of telephone customer service.
- The hours of operation and service availability for behavioral health care reflect the needs of members needing behavioral health care.

Member Satisfaction

Member satisfaction is analyzed by reviewing complaints, appeals, and requests to change providers. While not addressed in this standard, member satisfaction surveys are reviewed for evidence of compliance. Examples of member satisfaction accreditation standards are:

The managed care organization assesses member satisfaction by:

- evaluating member complaints and appeals, and
- evaluating requests to change practitioners and/or sites.

Utilization Management

Utilization management standards that are concerned with customer service include timeliness for appeals and satisfaction with the utilization management process.

Appeals

An **appeal** is a request to change a previous decision made by the organization. The appeals standards are quite detailed and involve notification, documentation, and resolution of appeals. There are two levels of appeals with timeliness standards for each and a requirement that an independent review organization be available to review. Appeals timeliness standards vary depending on whether the appeal is standard or expedited. Following are examples of appeals standards.

- The managed care organization has written policies and procedures for the thorough, appropriate, and timely resolution of member appeals.
- The managed care organization demonstrated compliance with the following:
  - appeals policies and procedures, and
  - member service instructions or standard operating procedures.

Member Satisfaction

Member and provider satisfaction with the utilization management process is assessed at least annually using satisfaction surveys. The utilization management process includes timeliness of care, appeals, denials, and clinical practice guidelines.

Examples of member satisfaction standards are:

- The managed care organization evaluates member and practitioner satisfaction with the utilization management process.
- At least annually, the managed care organization gathers information from the members and practitioners regarding their satisfaction with the utilization management process.
- The managed care organization addresses identified sources of dissatisfaction.

Members' Rights and Responsibilities

There are three standards under members' rights and responsibilities that address customer service. The first two are concerned with members understanding their rights and responsibilities. The last one is concerned with members' right to file a complaint.

The standards are quite specific on the minimum criteria for members' rights. In fact, many managed care organizations use NCQA's standard language verbatim and publish it in their member handbook or mail it out as a member rights brochure. Examples of members' rights standards are:

1. The managed care organization has a written policy that states the organization's commitment to treating members in a manner that respects their rights as well as its expectations of members' responsibilities. This policy addresses the following rights and responsibilities:
   - Members have the right to receive information about the managed care organization, its services, its practitioners and providers, and members' rights and responsibilities.

- Members have a right to be treated with respect and recognition of their dignity and right to privacy.

- Members have a right to participate with practitioners in decision making regarding their health care.

- Members have a right to a candid discussion of appropriate or medically necessary treatment options for their conditions, regardless of cost or benefit coverage.

- Members have a right to voice complaints or appeals about the managed care organization or the care provided.

- Members have a responsibility to provide, to the extent possible, information that the managed care organization and its practitioners and providers need in order to care for them.

- Members have a responsibility to follow the plans and instructions for care that they have agreed on with their practitioners.

2. The managed care organization distributes the policy on members' rights and responsibilities to members and participating practitioners.

While standards for appeals are addressed extensively in utilization management, the main focus in members' rights is on the complaint process. A complaint is an oral or written expression of dissatisfaction. Appeals are addressed at the policy level only as they relate to the right of a member to appeal the outcome of a decision.

Example:

- The managed care organization has written policies and procedures for the thorough, appropriate and timely resolution of member complaints and appeals.

Documentation Surveyed

During the accreditation survey, the surveyors will review the following documentation for evidence of compliance.

- availability standards,
- satisfaction surveys,
- complaint files and reports,
- QI reports,
- committee minutes,
- access plan,
- policy statements,
- CAHPS findings,
- primary care physician change reports,
- practitioner satisfaction surveys,
- member complaint analysis,

- practitioner complaint analysis,
- other documented member or practitioner feedback,
- statement of member rights and responsibilities,
- contracts between MCO and practitioners,
- member handbook and other communications,
- complaint and appeal policies and procedures, and
- member services instructions or standard operating procedures.

Source: www.ncqa.org

Review Questions

1. List and describe URAC's Core Standards that address customer service issues and services.

   _____
   _____
   _____
   _____

2. What is the responsibility of URAC's Quality Management Committee?

   _____
   _____
   _____
   _____

3. If a customer has registered a complaint or grievance with an organization, what does URAC require that the customer be entitled to receive in response?

   _____
   _____
   _____
   _____

4. What is the difference between a complaint and an appeal?

   _____
   _____
   _____
   _____

5. How is member satisfaction measured?

   _____
   _____
   _____
   _____

6. Name a responsibility that members have.

   _____
   _____
   _____
   _____

7. What is the difference between accessibility and availability?

_____

_____

_____

_____

8. Where does JCAHO address customer/patient service issues?

_____

_____

_____

_____

9. What is the goal of the rights and ethics function of the JCAHO standards?

_____

_____

_____

_____

10. What kind of information does JCAHO collect to ensure that customer/patient service issues are being addressed?

_____

_____

_____

_____

29

How Accreditation Affects Customer Service

Objectives

- Identify ways health care organizations comply with customer service standards.

- Learn how health plans collect information from consumers.

- Understand what surveyors look for when reviewing customer complaints and appeals processes.

- Know about criteria accrediting agencies use for assessing readability of health plan materials.

Now that we have covered accreditation and how it works, let's look at how accreditation impacts customer service. While this book discusses many ways to serve the customer, the accreditation process focuses on three aspects of customer service:

- satisfaction surveys,
- communicating member/consumer rights, and
- appeals and grievance procedures.

These three components are valid demonstrations of the impact that accreditation has on improving customer service. This chapter will refer to prior sections of the text and select illustrations from the various accrediting agencies that validate the contribution of accreditation to customer service.

Customer Service: Your Most Important Product

Service is produced at the time the product/service is delivered to the customer.

In health care, the *service produced* can refer to many things: a visit to a facility, patient, or provider; delivery of an item; or a phone call to a customer service call center.

NCQA uses a member satisfaction survey (CAHPS®) that asks members questions about how satisfied they are with their care in the following categories:

- courteous and helpful office staff,
- customer service,
- getting care quickly,
- getting needed care,
- how well doctors communicate, and
- claims processing.

Below are some examples of questions and results from the CAHPS® survey.

- In the last 12 months, how often were office staff at a doctor's office or clinic as helpful as you thought they should be? *89.1 percent said usually or always.*

- How often did office staff at a doctor's office or clinic treat you with courtesy and respect? *94.1 percent said usually or always.*

- In the last 12 months, how much of a problem, if any, was it to get the help you needed when you called your health plan's customer service? *84.6 percent said usually or always.*

- In the last 12 months, how often did you wait in the doctor's office or clinic more than 15 minutes past your appointment time to see the person you went to see? *34.9 percent said usually or always.*

URAC standards require that the organization have a method(s) to collect information about consumer satisfaction and that it utilize the method(s) on a regular basis. The standards also require that the organization have internal standards to assure that customers can receive services (often called performance benchmarks), with procedures in place to monitor the actual performance of the organization against the benchmarks. If benchmarks are not met, the organization needs to have a process in place to improve customer service. *Source: www.urac.org*

JCAHO's rights and ethics function seeks to "help improve patient outcomes by recognizing and respecting patients' rights during the provision of care or services. . ." *Source: www.jcaho.org*

Amends must sometimes be made for services or decisions that have been rendered.

The appeals and grievance policies and procedures that all accreditation agencies require serve to make amends for services or decisions that have been rendered. The services or decisions may have been made by a health plan, a provider, or provider staff. All three agencies require a process that allows a member to file a formal complaint about services received. The complaint may be about how they were treated, about the length of time it took to resolve an issue, or any other situation.

A member or consumer who wants a decision reversed would engage the appeals process. All agencies require that health plans have a process whereby a member or consumer can ask that a treatment or coverage decision be reversed. There are strict timeliness guidelines that correspond to the situation. For example, a decision that is retrospective in nature does not need to be addressed as urgently as a decision that impacts a member that is currently being treated.

Following are examples of verbiage from the various agencies' web sites regarding the complaints and appeals requirements.

- URAC—The organization has a system in place to receive and respond to consumer complaints as well as a process (often called grievance process) that allows customers to take additional steps if they are not satisfied with the initial decision or action taken on their complaint.

- JCAHO—The patient has the right to have complaints heard, reviewed, and, if possible, resolved.

- NCQA—Members have a right to voice complaints or appeals about the managed care organization or the care provided.

Quality service is a subjective issue.

The accrediting agencies seek to address the subjectivity of a person's experience by recognizing that individuals have differing needs based on their culture, language, gender, and other variables. The following standards are examples of this.

- NCQA—In creating and maintaining its delivery system of practitioners, the managed care organization takes into consideration assessed special and cultural needs and preferences.

- JCAHO—Be considerate of the patient's personal, cultural, and ethnic preferences.

- JCAHO—Staff should communicate with the patient in a language or form understandable to him or her taking into consideration communication barriers related to expressive aphasia, deafness, blindness, non-English speaking and/or limited education.

Taking Down the Seven Barriers to Outstanding Customer Service

The seven barriers to outstanding service were discussed in Part One, Chapter Four. Two of these barriers are addressed by accrediting agencies:

- a failure to coordinate all services, and
- the top priority being cost containment.

URAC has a standard that addresses the failure to coordinate all services:

The Organization has established and implemented mechanisms to promote coordination and communication across departments and disciplines within the Organization. The emphasis is to ensure integration of administrative activities, clinical operations and quality improvement.

One of the founding intentions of NCQA was to encourage health care plans to compete on quality and value, rather than price and provider network. This is clearly consistent with not having cost-containment be the top priority.

Strategies for Delivering Quality Service

Know what the customer wants.

The technique that accrediting agencies review to ensure that managed care organizations and health care providers are finding out what the customer wants is the use of customer satisfaction surveys. The JCAHO standard and its intent clearly define the context for understanding customer wants.

The organization collects patient perception of care data to monitor its performance.

Intent: JCAHO requires that data be collected on the needs, expectations, and satisfaction of individuals and organizations served as information gathered from patients and family members can provide insight about process design and functioning. The organization can use a number of ways to receive input from these groups including satisfaction surveys, regularly scheduling meetings with these groups, and focus groups.

Offer to help your customer.

All health plans have member service departments. These operate like call centers where members can call to have questions answered, find providers, replace ID cards, and take care of a myriad of other needs. NCQA requires that health plans establish standards for key elements of telephone customer service. Standards might include hold times, abandonment rates, and how fast the call is picked up.

Admit when you are wrong.

By having a complaint process in place, health care organizations have the ability to learn about problems with the system and to correct them. Frequently complaints can be handled with one phone call. An example might be if a member feels that a health care provider was rude, or the wait time was too long and the member wants to change providers. By following the complaint process, actions can be taken to assign a new provider, and, if the situation warrants, conduct a further investigation.

The other mechanism that health plans and facilities use to correct their actions is the appeals process. The appeals process is designed to correct decisions. Sometimes decisions on coverage or treatment are made, and then new information is introduced that indicates that the original decision should be reversed. Sometimes a closer look reveals that care that was originally denied should be delivered.

All accrediting agencies require processes and procedures for handling complaints and appeals.

Providing Outstanding Customer Service by Improving Customer Communication

Speak in a language the customer will understand.

One of the most frustrating aspects experienced by people needing medical attention is the difficulty understanding the steps the insurer requires in order to receive care. Insurance policies are written as legal contracts, and as such are often difficult to understand. Health plans now produce member handbooks that explain procedures in terms that are easier to understand.

On the health care delivery side, it can be equally frustrating, and frightening, to have a health care provider explain test results in technical terms. Many lay people do not understand what is being said or the implications of their illness or treatment. To address this issue, JCAHO has developed these standards.

- The patient is informed of his or her rights in a manner, which he or she understands.

- The patient has the right to have communication needs met.

- Staff should communicate with the patient in a language or form understandable to him or her taking into consideration communication barriers related to expressive aphasia, deafness, blindness, non-English speaking and/or limited education.

The CAHPS© survey shows that in 2000 93.2 percent of respondents felt that doctors or other health providers always or usually explained things in a way that they could understand. (NCQA's 2001 State of Managed Care Report)

Provide written information about services or products.

As noted above, health plans use member handbooks to communicate information that members need to know in order to use the health plan effectively. Additionally, health plans distribute information on members' rights to all plan participants. One of the criteria NCQA uses to assess the readability of health plan materials is that they be written to an eighth-grade level of understanding. The following standards from URAC and NCQA are examples of how accrediting agencies address this area.

- URAC—The Organization has a communications plan to inform consumers of their rights and responsibilities.

- NCQA—The managed care organization distributes the policy on members' rights and responsibilities to members and participating practitioners.

Information from a composite of all health plan responses to the CAHPS® survey shows that 57.1 percent of respondents felt that it was not a problem to find information in the health plan's written materials; 33.6 percent said it was a small problem; and 9.2 percent indicated that it was a big problem. (*Source: Health Choices Web Site*)

Provide the essential contact information.

Accrediting agencies require health plans to have standards for routine, urgent, and emergency care, including instructions to call 911 in an emergency. These standards are communicated in the member handbook and usually the ID card as well.

Verifying the Quality of Service

Provide each customer with a customer service survey form.

Surveying each customer about his or her experience would be cost prohibitive. Most health care organizations use a third party to survey a percentage of members. Since the surveying party is not associated with the health plan, the results are blind so there is no concern over confidentiality. In addition, if a member has a complaint and is not one of those randomly selected to participate in the survey, the member can follow the complaint process described earlier.

Ask customers what they would recommend for improving service.

Both URAC and NCQA gather input from customer surveys; however, JCAHO has a very comprehensive program that includes a mechanism for obtaining public feedback during a survey. JCAHO isn't only looking at closed-end questions or rating scales of satisfaction, it is also proactively looking for expectations and satisfaction with the whole process of treatment and care. To obtain more of a 360-degree view of the health care organization, JCAHO invites feedback from patients and their families as well as referral sources and the community at large.

When Nothing Seems to Work

Keep communicating with your customer.

All accrediting agencies have timeliness requirements for the appeals and grievance processes. Generally, these types of communications are the most volatile. The timeliness requirements ensure that the member is communicated with on a timeline appropriate to the situation. For urgent situations the turnaround time on decisions can be 24–48 hours. For situations that are less urgent, or when appealing claims that have been denied, the turnaround time may be 30 days or more. The member is advised of the timeliness standards in the member handbook and in writing at the time an appeal is filed.

Criteria for Evaluating the Quality of Service

Communication

As noted previously, accrediting agencies require health plans to communicate with members in a manner that they understand. Having materials written to an eighth-grade level, and in languages that account for more than 10 percent of the population, are examples of how health plans comply with this requirement.

Responsiveness

The timeliness standards for phone calls, office wait times, and utilization management decisions are all designed so that health care services are rendered on an appropriate schedule. Having accelerated standards for urgent and emergency situations ensures that treatment and decision times are appropriate to the situation.

Knowing and understanding the customer

Satisfaction surveys are the primary source of information that health plans use to receive customer feedback. Additionally, when health plans are designing a new program, such as a diabetes management program, they will set up focus groups with potential users to understand their needs and design the program around the stated needs. Some plans also develop pilot programs where they will roll out a new program or product to a limited number of people and revise the program based on feedback.

Review Questions

1. What are the three most common ways health care organizations comply with customer service standards?

   _____

   _____

   _____

   _____

2. How do health plans most often collect information from consumers?

   _____

   _____

   _____

   _____

3. What process is used if a customer is unhappy with the service received?

   _____

   _____

   _____

   _____

4. What process is used to reverse coverage decisions?

   _____

   _____

   _____

   _____

5. What are the special needs that managed care organizations take into consideration in order to make sure they are communicating with members in a way that is understandable?

   _____

   _____

   _____

   _____

6. Which agency seeks input from the public during its survey process?

   _____

   _____

   _____

   _____

Appendix A
50 Tips for Quality Customer Service

This is a working list for you and your colleagues to discuss and add to as you develop your customer service program. The list provides reminders of the many issues discussed in *Customer Service Strategies for the Health Care Environment*. Review each item and think about how it relates to you and your business. Discuss the tips and determine whether you follow the recommendations and what you can do to improve the quality of your services.

1. Always thank customers for their business.

2. Treat customers as if you were related to them.

3. Thank customers for calling.

4. Use your first and last name when speaking with customers.

5. Do not get angry with the customer.

6. Keep your promises.

7. Treat all messages as business orders.

8. Never say "I don't know" without attempting to locate the answers.

9. Keep to your schedule of appointments.

10. Remember: Customers are the reason you are in business.

11. Customer service is everyone's responsibility.

12. Allow customers to express their anger.

13. Verify all customer information.

14. Provide customers with emergency contact information.

15. Provide a business card to all customers.

16. Call to follow up on all services.

17. Respect the dignity of all customers.

18. Take the extra steps to make customers happy.

19. Make the customer feel important.

20. Send thank you notes for all business received.

21. Do not let long-term customers think they have been forgotten.

22. When closing a conversation, verify all information the customer has given you.

23. Put the time and date on all messages you receive.

24. Be accessible to your customers.

25. Do not make a customer wait on the telephone without asking permission.

26. Never blame the company for a customer service problem.

27. Under promise and over deliver.

28. Understand that people do business with people they like.

29. Apologize with sincerity.

30. Offer to help all customers.

31. Apologize for any unexpected delays.

32. Be both health care product/service provider and customer educator.

33. Take ownership of all company complaints.

34. Avoid saying, "It's not my department."

35. Throughout all times of the day, treat customers with the same enthusiasm.

36. Explain and provide additional information to all customers.

37. Take pride in your work and your product.

38. Do not belittle a customer's feelings.

39. Apologize for failing to keep to a schedule.

40. Pick up all telephone calls by the third ring.

41. Help the customer understand all issues related to the services you provide.

42. Promise to share what you have done to resolve the customer's complaint.

43. Never tell the customer "It's no problem."

44. Never make promises for another employee.

45. Take all complaints seriously.

46. Take the extra time to repeat all instructions.

47. When speaking with a customer, talk with assurance.

48. See the customer as your best public relations agent.

49. Never view customers as an interruption in your workday; they are the reason you have a job.

50. **Remember, people do business with people who are easy to do business with.**

Appendix B

Accreditations Available by Accrediting Agency

Joint Commission on Accreditation of Healthcare Organizations (JCAHO)[1]

JCAHO provides evaluation and accreditation services for the following types of organizations:

- Ambulatory care providers, including outpatient surgery facilities, rehabilitation centers, infusion centers, group practices and others
- Assisted living facilities that provide or coordinate personal services, 24-hour supervision and assistance (scheduled and unscheduled), activities and health-related services
- Behavioral health care organizations, including those that provide mental health and addiction services, and services to persons with developmental disabilities of various ages, in various organized service settings
- Clinical and pathology laboratories
- General, psychiatric, children's and rehabilitation hospitals
- Health care networks, including health maintenance organizations (HMOs), integrated delivery networks (IDNs), preferred provider organizations (PPOs), and managed behavioral health care organizations
- Home care organizations, including those that provide home health services, personal care and support services, home infusion and other pharmacy services, durable medical equipment services and hospice services
- Nursing homes and other long-term care facilities, including subacute care programs; dementia programs and long-term care pharmacies

National Committee for Quality Assurance (NCQA)[2]

- Credentials Verification Organizations (Certification)
- Disease Management

---

[1] ©Joint Commission: *2001-2002 Standards Manual for Home Health, Personal Care, Support Services.* Oakbrook Terrace, IL: Joint Commission on Accreditation of Healthcare Organizations, 2001, pp. 64-72, 73-75.

[2] National Committee for Quality Assurance. *Surveyor Guidelines for the Accreditation of MCOs.* Washington: NCQA, 2001. Reprinted with Permission.

- Managed Care Organizations
- Managed Behavioral Health Care Organizations
- New Health Plans
- Physician Organization (Certification)
- Preferred Provider Organizations
- Utilization Management and Credentialing (Certification)

Utilization Review Accreditation Commission (URAC)[3]

- Case Management Accreditation
- Claims Processing Accreditation
- Core Accreditation
- Credential Verification Organization (CVO) Accreditation
- Disease Management Accreditation (under development)
- External Review Organization Accreditation
- Health Call Center Accreditation
- Health Network Accreditation
- Health Plan Accreditation
- Health Utilization Management Accreditation
- Health Provider Credentialing Accreditation
- Health Web Site Accreditation
- Workers' Compensation Network Accreditation
- Workers' Compensation Utilization Management Accreditation

[3] Source: www.uarc.org/programs/core.htm Reprinted with Permission from URAC (also known as the American Accreditation HealthCare Commission).

Appendix C
Overview by Accrediting Agency of the Major Standard Areas

Joint Commission on Accreditation of Healthcare Organizations (JCAHO)[1]

Performance relates to the ability of an organization to carry out those key organizational or patient care functions most important to achieving quality results. These key functions comprise organizational processes and systems and are categorized as those functions directly related to patient care or those functions that support patient care. In turn, these functions are the basis for the JCAHO standards and comprise the actual chapters of the various manuals.

Patient-Focused Functions

1. Rights and Ethics
2. Assessment
3. Care, Treatment, and Services
4. Education
5. Continuum of Care

Organization Functions

1. Improving Organization Performance
2. Leadership
3. Environmental Safety and Equipment Management
4. Management of Human Resources
5. Management of Information
6. Surveillance, Prevention and Control of Infection

[1] ©Joint Commission: *2001-2002 Standards Manual for Home Health, Personal Care, Support Services*. Oakbrook Terrace, IL: Joint Commission on Accreditation of Healthcare Organizations, 2001, pp. 64-72, 73-75. Reprinted with Permission.

National Committee for Quality Assurance (NCQA)[2]
Quality Improvement (QI) Processes

1. Quality Improvement Program Structure
2. Quality Improvement Program Operations
3. Physician Contract Requirements
4. Availability of Practitioners
5. Accessibility of Services
6. Member Satisfaction
7. Assistance for People with Chronic Health Conditions
8. Clinical Practice Guidelines
9. Continuity and Coordination of Care
10. Clinical Measurement Activities
11. Intervention and Follow-up for Clinical Issues
12. Effectiveness of the QI Program
13. Delegation of QI Activity

Processes for Reviewing and Authorizing Medical Care

1. Utilization Management Structure
2. Clinical Criteria for UM Decisions
3. Appropriate Professionals
4. Timeliness of Medical Review Decisions
5. Medical Information
6. Denial Notices
7. Evaluation of New Technology
8. Satisfaction with the UM Process
9. Emergency Services
10. Procedures for Pharmaceutical Management
11. Ensuring Appropriate Service and Coverage
12. Triage and Referral for Behavioral Health Care
13. Delegation of UM

Quality of Provider Network

1. Credentialing Policies
2. Credentialing Committee

---

[2] National Committee for Quality Assurance. *Surveyor Guidelines for the Accreditation of MCOs*. Washington: NCQA, 2001. Reprinted with Permission.

3. Initial Primary Source Verification

4. Application and Attestation

5. Initial Sanction Information

6. Initial Credentialing Site Visits

7. Recredentialing Primary Source Verification

8. Recredentialing Sanction Information

9. Performance Monitoring

10. Practitioner Appeal Rights

11. Assessment of Organizational Providers

12. Delegation of Credentialing

Members' Rights and Responsibilities

1. Statement of Members' Rights and Responsibilities

2. Distribution of Rights Statements to Members and Practitioners

3. Policies for Complaints and Appeals

4. Appropriate Handling of Complaints and Appeals

5. Subscriber Information

6. Privacy and Confidentiality

7. Marketing Information

8. Delegation of Members' Rights and Responsibilities

Preventive Health Activities

1. Adoption of Preventive Health Guidelines

2. Distribution of Guidelines to Practitioners

3. Health Promotion with Members

4. Delegation of PH

Medical Records

1. Medical Record Documentation Standards

Utilization Review Accreditation Commission (URAC)[3]

As previously noted, URAC currently has 12 accreditations available, each with a unique set of standards related to the type of accreditation. However, the following Core Standards for Organizational Quality are consistent within these accreditations:

---

[3] Source: www.urac.org/programs/core.htm. Reprinted with Permission from URAC (also known as the American Accreditation HealthCare Commission).

1. Standards for Administration
   - Policies and Procedures
   - Inter-department Coordination
   - Information Management
   - Oversight of Delegated/Sub-contracted Functions
   - Business Relationships

2. Standards for Staffing
   - Staff Qualifications
   - Staff Management
   - Clinical Oversight
   - Organizational Management

3. Standards for Confidentiality
   - Confidentiality Policies and Procedures
   - Staff Training and Oversight

4. Standards for Consumer Protection
   - Consumer and Patient Safety
   - Financial Incentives
   - Communications*
   - Satisfaction*
   - Ability of Consumers to Obtain Services*
   - Complaints and Grievances*
   - *Note: apply only to organizations that have direct contact with consumers

5. Quality Management
   - Quality Management Plan
   - Quality Management Committee
   - Quality Management Program
   - Quality Improvement Projects

Notes

Anderson, K., and R. Zemke. *Delivering Knock Your Socks Off Service*. New York: American Management Association, 1998.

Blanchard, Kenneth H., and Sheldon Bowles. *Raving Fans: A Revolutionary Approach to Customer Service*. New York: Morrow & Co.,1993.

Chesla, Erik. *Successful Teamwork*. Chicago: Learning Express Publishers, 1999.

Davidow, William H., and Bro Uttal. *Total Customer Service: The Utmost Weapon*. New York: Harper & Row Publishers, 1989.

Donnelly, James H. *25 Management Lessons from the Customer's Side of the Counter*. Toronto: Irwin Professional Publishing, 1989.

Fisher, Kimball. *Leading Self-Directed Work Teams: A Guide to Developing New Team Leadership Skills*. New York: McGraw-Hill, 2000.

Gage, Susan M. *The Agile Manager's Guide to Extraordinary Customer Service*. Vermont: Velocity Business Publishing, 1999.

Gee, Jeff, and Val Gee. *Super Service*. New York: McGraw-Hill, 1999.

Gross, T. Scott. *Outrageous Unforgettable Service . . . Guilt-Free Selling*. New York: American Management Association, 1998.

Gummer, B. "Power, Power, Who's Got the Power?" *Administration in Social Work* 9:2 (1985): 99-111.

Heit, Gary, Tom Parker, and Deborah C. Stephens. *One Size Fits One, Second Edition*. New York: John Wiley & Sons, Inc., 1999.

Johnston, Bernice. *Real World Customer Service*. Naperville: SourceBooks, Inc., 1996.

Joint Commission: *2001-2002 Standards Manual for Home Health, Personal Care, Support Services*. Oakbrook Terrace, IL: Joint Commission on Accreditation of Healthcare Organizations, 2001, pp. 64-72, 73-75.

Jolles, Robert L. *Customer Center Selling*. New York: The Free Press, 1998.

Leland, Karen, and Keith Bailey. *Customer Service for Dummies, 2nd Edition*. Chicago: IDG Books Worldwide, Inc., 1999.

Maddus, B., and Elwood N. Chapman. *Your First Thirty Days–Revised: Building a Professional Image in a New Job*. Menlo Park: Crisp Publications, 1997.

Morgan, Rebecca L. *Calming Upset Customers, Revised Edition*. Menlo Park: Crisp Publications, Inc. California, 1986.

National Committee for Quality Assurance. *Surveyor Guidelines for the Accreditation of MCOs*. Washington: NCQA, 2001.

Taylor, Don, and Jeanne Smalling Archer. *Up Against the Walmarts*. New York: American Management Association, 1994.

Timm, Paul R. *50 Powerful Ideas You Can Use to Keep Your Customers*. Franklin Lakes: Career Press, 1995.

URAC's Core Standards from URAC's Web Site (*www.urac.org/programs/core.htm*). Washington: URAC (also known as the American Accreditation HealthCare Commission), 2002.

Wax, John. "Power Theory and Institutional Change." *Social Science Review* 66 (Spring 1971): 274-289.

Wilner, Jack. *7 Secrets to Successful Sales Management: The Sales Manager's Manual.* Boca Raton: St. Lucie Press,1998.

Wing, Michael. *Talking With Your Customers.* Menlo: Upstart Publishing, 1997.

Zemke, Ron, and Dick Schaaf. *The Service Edge.* Chicago: Lakewood Publishers, 1989.

Key Terms

Accessibility, 206

Account assessment system, 69

Account assessment, 36

Accreditation process, 174

Accreditation standards, 171

Accreditation, 171

American Accreditation Healthcare Commission, 172

Amiable negotiator, 116

Analyst, 115

Annual customer report, 72

Antagonists, 110

Availability, 206

CAHPS®, 178

Chart or record reviews, 175

Checklist, 85

Complaint report, 151

Conditional accreditation, 175

Consumer Assessment of Health Plans Study (CAHPS), 176

Core standards for organization quality, 199

Cost containment, 28

Customer education materials, 54

Customer needs assessment, 70

Customer service cycle, 84

Customer-friendly systems, 4

Customer-oriented people, 4

Denial, 175

Documentation review, 174

Extrovert, 115

Face-to-face meetings, 72

Flowchart, 84

Followers, 108

Full accreditation, 175

Golden rule, 12

Health Plan Employer Data and Information Set (HEDIS®), 172

Health Plan Report Card, 173

Interviews, 174

Joint Commission of Accreditation of Healthcare Organizations (JCAHO), 172

Leaders, 108

Licensure, 171

Member satisfaction survey, 176

Member satisfaction, 206

National Committee on Quality Assurance (NCQA), 172

Organization chart, 70

ORYX™, 188

Performance benchmarks, 200

Planners, 109

Pramatic negotiator, 116

Product fact sheet, 64

Profit center, 40

Quality service, 4

Resisters, 109

Self-evaluation, 29

Service units, 83

State of Managed Care Quality Report, 178

Surveyors, 175

Team building, 108

Teams, 108

Telephone interviews, 70

Thinkers, 108

Utilization Review Accreditation Commission (URAC), 172

Win-win negotiation, 114

Index

accessibility, 10, 206
  NCQA, 193
account assessment, 36–37, 69–70
accreditation, 169–220
  conditional, 175
  customer service and, 213–220
  defined, 171
  denial, 175
  full, 175
  JCAHO, 186–187, 189–190
  NCQA, 192, 194
  objectives, 171, 213
  organizations, 172
  process, 174–175
  purpose, 171–182
  review questions, 182, 220
  survey, 187
  URAC, 184
  value of, 173–174
  value to customer service, 175–177
  value to health care delivery, 177
Accreditation Committee, URAC, 185
Accreditation Denied, 190
accreditation standards, 171–172, 199–211
  JCAHO, 201–205
  NCQA, 205–209
  objectives, 199
  review questions, 210–211
  URAC, 199–201
Accreditation with Type 1
    Recommendations, 190
Accreditation without Type 1
    Recommendations, 190
accredited, 194
accrediting bodies, 183–197, 223–224
  objectives, 183
  overview, 225–228
  review questions, 197
administration, 123–124
admit when you are wrong, 216–217
advance directives, 203
Agency for Healthcare Research and Quality
    (AHRQ), 176
Agenda for Change, 189

Albrecht, Karl, 141
amends, 214–215
American Accreditation Healthcare
    Commission, 172
analyst, 115–116
annual customer reports, 72
antagonists, 110
apology, 20, 45–46, 57–58
  checklist, 21
  written, 58, 59
appeals, 207
appearance, 89–90
assistance, offering, 43–44, 162, 216
assurance, 53
attitude, 129
availability, 206

barriers, 25–32
  list, 31
  objectives, 25
  review questions, 32
behavior, 37–38
blame
  complaints and, 150
  the system, 146
business habits, 12–13
business interactions, 17–19
  monitoring, 18
business philosophy, 3–6
  objectives, 3
  review questions, 6

CAHPS®. *See* Consumer Assessment of
    Health Plans Study
caregivers, 12–13
charisma, 114
chart reviews, 174
checklists, customer service cycle analysis,
    85
coding system, 124
commendable, 194
commitment
  customers', 8
  to customer service, 4, 134
communication, 22–23, 90, 200, 203,
    218–219
  comments to avoid, 155–159

continuing, 58, 60
improving, 217–218
objectives, 51, 155
review questions, 56, 159
terminology, 39–40
tools, 51–56
what you need to know first, 158
when nothing seems to work, 218
communicator, effective, 129
competence, 90
competition, 33–34
accreditation and, 180–181
competitors, 20, 80, 99
complaints, 30, 139–168, 201, 203
common, 145–148
concern, 163
impact of, 141–144
information from, 151
listening, 161
monitoring the handling of, 94
objectives, 141, 145, 149, 161
opportunity offered, 150
report, 151, 152
review questions, 144, 148, 153, 164
solutions, 161–164
source, 146–147
thanking the customer, 163
value of, 149–153
value received, 151
compromise, 114
The computer is down, 156
concentration, 66
concern, customer's complaint, 163
Conditional Accreditation, 190
conferences, URAC, 185
confidence, 117–118
confidentiality, 203
consistency, 11–12
Consumer Assessment of Health Plans Study®,
190, 191, 193–194, 214, 215, 217, 218
Consortium, 176
standards to improve health care, 179
consumers, 191
contacts, 54–55
developing and updating information,
124
evaluating, 23
number of, 22–23
stopped calling, 149
conviction, 117
coordination of services, 26–27, 200,
215–216
Core Standards for Organizational Quality,
199–201

cost containment, 28
courtesy, 12, 45, 90, 145
creativity, 129
customer-driven organization
creating, 3–6
objectives, 3
review questions, 6
customer-friendly systems, 4
customer-oriented people, 4
customers
acknowledging your customer's feelings,
46–47
angry, 19, 20, 142
attracting new ones vs keeping old ones,
143
calling, 78
conversations, 17–19
difficult, 58
education materials, 54
feedback, 103
help the customer understand the details,
60
interactions, 16–17
knowing and understanding, 35–37, 219
learning about, 69–73
loyalty, 141
needs, 22, 38–40
objectives, 69
response, 18
review questions, 73
satisfaction, 200
service committee, 100–101
service program, 5
special, 22
unhappy, 142–143
ways they can damage your business, 143
customer relationships
enhancement, 150
make the customer feel important, 41–42
reviewing, 19
customer service, 9–10, 75–96
as product, 15–24, 213–215
barriers to outstanding customer service,
215–217
extra, 58
impressive, 34
negative comments, 19
objectives, 7, 15
poor, 35
quality, 215
review questions, 14, 24
selling, 19
standards, 205–209
strategies, 216–217

subjectivity, 21
survey, 78–79
that makes a difference, 7–14
tips, 221–222
customer service cycle
analyzing, 83–87
creating, 86
defined, 84
objectives, 83
review questions, 87
Customer Service Strategies for the Health Care Environment, 134

damage control, 18
data collection, 204, 216
decision makers, 270
negotiation and, 119
decision making, 202–203
customer, 162
delivery, 16
demeanor, 17
Deming, W. Edwards, 142
demographics, customer survey, 78
denied, 194
directory, company, 64
documentation, 103–104, 217–218
review, 174
surveyed, 208–209
documents, negotiation, 121
Drucker, Peter, 141–142

education
in-service needs, 90
URAC, 185
see also training
efficiency, 123–126
objectives, 123
review questions, 126
employees
acknowledgment, 12
customer service philosophy, 30
feedback, 101
hiring, 127–132
indifferent and unmotivated, 28–29
see also training
employers, 191
endurance, 117
escape clause, 120
ethics, organization, 204
evaluation
competitors' service, 80
criteria, 89–92
objectives, 89
review questions, 92

excellence, 194
excuses, 63–64
expectations, exceeding, 12, 13
experience, 29, 128
extroverts, 115

feedback
customers, 103
employees, 101, 136–137
feelings, 16
fees, URAC, 186
fence-sitters, 110
files management, 123–124
flowchart, 84, 117, 129
followers, 108–109
follow-through, 8

gag clauses, 177
getting better, NCQA, 193
glossary, creating, 39–40
goal-oriented, 129
gratitude, 44
check 44
growth potential, 128

health care practices, 191
Health Plan Employer Data and Information
Set (HEDIS®), 172, 173, 190, 191,
192, 193–194
standards to improve health care, 177–178
Health Plan Report Card, 173
health plans, 191
help. *See* assistance
hidden agendas, 119
hiring, 127–132
avoiding the wrong person, 129–131
finding the right person, 128–129
objectives, 127
review questions, 132
see also employees
honesty, 42
human resources departments, 173–174

I don't know, 155–156
I have never heard of that happening, 158
I'll do the best I can, 155
I'll look into it, 156
improvement, 194–195
improvement
performance, 204–205
quality, 205–206
industry trends, 30
information
accessibility, 125

confirm that the caller has it correctly, 162
negotiation, 114, 115
power, 115
provision, monitoring, 95
services and products, written, 54
written, 217–218
informing patients, 202
innovativeness, 129
instruction manuals, 95
integrity, 60
interviews, 174
face-to-face, 72
It's not my department, 156
It's not my job, 3

jobs
descriptions, 200
evaluation, your own, 131
Joint Commission of Accreditation of Healthcare Organizations (JCAHO), 172,
173, 174, 175, 176, 186–190, 214,
215, 216, 218, 223
accreditation decision, 189–190
accreditation services, 186–187
accreditation survey, 187
governance, 186
measurement, 187–189
organization functions, 225
patient-focused functions, 225
standards, 179, 187–189, 201–205, 225
survey process, 189

knowledge. *See* product knowledge

language, 217
leaders, 108
leadership, 30
licensure, 171
limited victory, 118
listening, 161, 165
active, 38
colleagues, 29
techniques, 38
living with illness, NCQA, 193
location, 11
lying, 42

managed care, 207–208
management, 99–105, 141–142
objectives, 99
review questions, 105
marketplace
evaluation, 30

skills, 30
understanding, 35–37
Medicare certification, accreditation, 181
meetings, 101
face-to-face, 72
members
rights and responsibilities, 207–208
satisfaction, 206, 207
survey, 176, 214
messages, 65–66
mistakes
acknowledging, 57
admitting when you are wrong, 45–46
monitoring problem areas, 93–96
objectives, 93
review questions, 96

National Committee on Quality Assurance
(NCQA), 172, 173, 174, 175, 176,
177, 190–195, 217, 218, 223–224
accreditation, 194
accreditation process, 192
medical records, 227
members' rights and responsibilities, 227
performance criteria, 193
preventive health activities, 227
quality cycle, 194–195
quality improvement, 226
quality of provider network, 226–227
reviewing and authorizing care, 226
scoring, 193–194
stakeholders, 191
standards, 177–179, 205–209, 226–227
survey process, 192
needs, 114
assessment, 70, 99
employees, 127–128
negotiation, 113–122
critical elements, 114–115
objectives, 113
pitfalls, 120–121
review questions, 122
stages, 114
strategies for winning, 119–120
styles, 115–116
understanding, 118–119
win-win, 113–114
your style, 116
negotiator
amiable, 116
good, 117–119
mind of, 118–119

Official Accreditation Decision Report, 189
on-time delivery, monitoring, 93–94

operationalism, accreditation and, 181
organization
    chart, 70, 119
    negotiation and, 119
    size and customer service, 7
    structure, 200
ORYX®, 188

patience, 37
patients, 13
    perception, 216
    rights, 201–203
People do business with people they like, 8
People do business with people who are
        easy to do business with, 10, 55
people skills, 127
performance
    benchmarks, 200–201
    criteria, 193
    improving, 204–205
    JCAHO, 187–188
    measurement, 188
    NCQA, 193
    standards, 187–188
planners, 109
policies, 199–200
    control and convenience of the
        organization, 25–26
    evaluating, 26
    revision, 104, 157
policy makers, 191
power, 114–115
pragmatic negotiator, 116
preferred business, becoming, 8–9
Preliminary Denial of Accreditation, 190
preliminary report, 175
priorities, negotiation, 121
privacy, 203
problems, 57–61
    course of action, 166–167
    entire, 161
    objectives, 57
    options for correcting, 166
    passing to someone else, 146
    pinpointing, 146–147
    primary, 165
    repeat it, 162
    review questions, 61
    understand, identify, discuss, and agree,
        167
problem solving, 143
    action plan, 162–163
    exercise, 167
    monitoring, 94

objectives, 165
    resolution, 150
    review questions, 168
    strategies, 165–168
procedures, 199–200
    testing, 103, 108
product fact sheets, 64
product knowledge, 15, 118
products, verifying that you have given
        correct information, 77–78
profit center, 40–41
program director, 100
promises, 26, 42–43
    not kept, 145–146
provisional, 194
Provisional Accreditation, 190
public information
    interview, 204–205
    policy, 205
publications, URAC, 185

qualified providers, NCQA, 193
quality cycle, NCQA, 194–195
quality management program, 201
quality of service, 4
    evaluating, 218–219
    interpretation, 16–17
    objectives, 77
    review questions, 81
    subjectivity, 21
    verifying, 77–81, 218
questioning the customer, 38–40
questions
    frequently asked, 36, 52
    encourage customers to ask, 52

rating your company, 90
reality check, 8–9
recommendations, 218
    customer service standards, 103
    improving service, 80
record reviews, 174
referral sources, 13
reliability, 90
reminders, 11
reporting, monitoring, 94
research, URAC, 185
resisters, 109–110
respect, 117–118
responsiveness, 90, 219
review, URAC, 186
rewards, understanding, 119

scoring
    JCAHO, 188–189

NCQA, 193–194
security, 203
self-evaluation, 29
service, 16
    produced, 213–214
    strategies, 134
    verifying that you have given correct
        information, 77–78
service units, defined, 83
shouting, 165
    How do I feel?, 166
simplicity, 10, 22–23
sincerity, 10
skill set, 128
special needs, 22
stakeholders, NCQA, 191
standards, 101–102
    CAHPS®, 179
    customer service, 205–209
    examples, 177–180
    explaining, 30
    HEDIS®, 177–178
    JCAHO, 179, 187–189, 225
    NCQA, 177–179, 226–227
    URAC, 179–180, 227–228
State of Managed Care Quality Report, 178
state of mind, service and, 37–38
staying healthy, NCQA, 193
strategies, 33–48
    objectives, 33
    review questions, 48
surveyor qualifications, 175
surveys, 78
    demographics, 78
    form, 218
    JCAHO, 189
    NCQA, 192
    process, 189, 192
    recommendations from, 71
    sample, 79
    telephone, 71–72
    written, 70

team-building, 107–111
    defined, 107–108
    objectives, 107
    review questions, 111
team members, 108–110
    contributions, 110
    who's who, 109
team player, 128–129
teams, defined, 107
technology, 10, 30
telephone calls, 78
    answering, 18, 65, 84–85

concentration, 66
    messages, 65–66
    monitoring the system, 65
    objectives, 63
    review questions, 67
    strategies, 63–67
telephone interviews, 71
terminology, 51–52
    customer service problems, 39–40
    difficult, 53
testing, process, 103
thank you's, 41, 44
    check, 44
That's not our policy, 156–157
That's the second time I have heard that, 156
thinkers, 108
threats, 120–121
time, 11–12
timing, 115
tone of voice, 53
tracking, monitoring, 94
training, 102–103, 104
    documentation, 136
    documentation form, 136
    employee survey form, 137
    employees' records, 135–136
    manual, 134
    objectives, 133
    program, 133–138
    review questions, 138
    sessions, 135
    see also education

understanding, 90
    asking for, 53
utilization management, standards, 206–208
Utilization Review Accreditation Commission
        (URAC), 172, 173, 174, 175–176, 183–
        186, 214, 215, 217, 218, 224
    accreditation process, 185–186
    organization, 183–184
    services, 184–185
    stakeholders and customers, 186
    standards, 179–180, 199–201, 227–228

victory, limited, 118
voice mail, 65

winning, components of, 119–120
win-win negotiating, 113–114
work habits, 125
work times, best and worst, 17

You should have told me that first, 157

Zemke, Ron, 141

Frequently Asked Questions
About the HIAA Examination

What material does the examination for the HIAA course Customer Service Strategies for the Health Care Environment cover?

The 29 chapters of the textbook *Customer Service Strategies for the Health Care Environment*.

Is information from appendices covered in the exam?

No. Appendices are provided as a resource for the reader. Any information that appears *only* in appendices (and not in the chapters of the text as well) is not tested.

How many questions are on the exam, and how much time do I have?

There are 75 questions. You have two hours to complete the exam.

What is the format of the questions of the exam?

All questions are multiple choice.

EXAMPLE

Every customer service team includes a variety of people who perform different roles. Planners are those who

a. *help others understand the process.*
b. *go along with the group without questioning.*
c. *help others look ahead and build a vision.*
d. *are quick to delegate.*

(*The correct answer is c.*)

Some questions are multiple-option multiple choice.

EXAMPLE

An accreditation survey generally includes

I. *a tour of the facility or office.*
II. *interviews with clinical leadership and staff.*

III. *review of charts and records.*

IV. *review of policies and procedures.*

    a. I and III only.

    b. II and IV only.

    c. I, II, and III only.

    d. I, II, III, and IV.

(The correct answer is d.)

A few questions are application questions. These require you to determine which of the facts given in the question are relevant and then apply your knowledge to reach a conclusion.

EXAMPLE

Jan Crouse has an excellent reputation for handling difficult customers at the call center where she works. Her company launched a new product and later discovered it had defects. When an irate customer calls to report problems, what is Jan's first course of action?

a. She puts the customer on hold while she researches the problem.

b. She transfers the call to John in the IT department who can fix the problem.

c. She apologizes and begins the process of winning the customer back.

d. She says, "We've been having a lot of problems with that product."

(The correct answer is c.)

You should be able to answer the question by applying your knowledge of customer service strategies that keep customers satisfied and coming back.

If I can answer all the review questions, will I be able to pass the exam?

Not necessarily. In this case the review questions are designed to help the student focus on key concepts covered in the text, but they do not cover everything that might be asked on the exam.

I have a lot of experience in customer service. Can I pass the exam without reading the textbook or studying?

Possibly, but you should be aware that the text covers a lot of topic areas. For example, this textbook covers management and training issues as they relate to customer service. You will also find a section devoted to accreditation that will help you gain a better understanding of what the three major accrediting organizations look for and how accreditation standards translate into better customer service. The safest approach is to read the textbook and see if you know the material. This will go very quickly if you already have a lot of knowledge.

HIAA's Courses and Professional Designations

For more than 40 years, the Health Insurance Association of America's Insurance Education Program has offered current, comprehensive, and economically priced courses for professionals seeking to advance their understanding of the health insurance industry. Since 1958, more than 500,000 people have enrolled in these courses. Many enrollees are employees of health insurance companies or managed care organizations, but consultants, third-party administrators, agents, brokers, and other health insurance professionals also study with us. In addition, an increasing number of noninsurance professionals, including health care providers, economists, consumer advocates, and government officials, are taking HIAA courses to gain a better understanding of the operations of our industry and to advance their careers in their own fields.

Courses include:

- The Fundamentals of Health Insurance (Parts A and B)

- Managed Care (Parts A, B, and C)

- Medical Expense Insurance

- Supplemental Health Insurance

- Disability Income Insurance

- Long-Term Care Insurance

- Financing Long-Term Care

- Health Insurance Fraud

- Customer Service for the Health Care Environment

The completion of HIAA courses leads to four widely respected professional designations: **Health Insurance Associate (HIA), Managed Healthcare Professional (MHP), Long-Term Care Professional (LTCP),** and the **Health Care Anti-Fraud Associate (HCAFA)**. The HIA designation has been in existence since 1990 and is currently held by more than 16,500 professionals. The MHP, offered for the first time in 1996, is held by more than 4,000 designees. The LTCP designation is currently being introduced.

And coming soon . . . additional courses and new designations in disability income and medical management.

For more information, visit our web site (www.hiaa.org) or call 800-509-4422.

Other Books from HIAA

Long-Term Care: Understanding Needs and Options

This book provides an introduction to the field of long-term care and long-term care insurance. It begins with an explanation of what long-term care is, who needs it, and how and where it is provided. It then looks at various ways of paying for long-term care and the limitations of each. It examines long-term care insurance, learning how it works and why it is often the best solution to the problem. Finally, it discusses the ways salespeople and insurance company personnel can bring this solution to the people who need it.

The Health Insurance Primer:
An Introduction to How Health Insurance Works

This book, together with *Health Insurance Nuts and Bolts*, serves as a complete introduction to the health insurance field. The authors assume no prior knowledge and begin by explaining basic concepts and terminology, but they progress to an in-depth examination of such topics as the various kinds of health insurance, health insurance contracts, underwriting, and sales and marketing. *The Health Insurance Primer* is an excellent choice for beginners in health insurance.

Health Insurance Nuts and Bolts:
An Introduction to Health Insurance Operations

The introduction to the basic facts and concepts of group and individual health insurance begun in *The Health Insurance Primer* continues in *Health Insurance Nuts and Bolts*. Topics include managing the cost of health care; policy issue, renewal, and service; claim administration; pricing health insurance products; government regulation; and fraud and abuse.

Medical Expense Insurance

For those who have a basic understanding of the concepts and functioning of health insurance, this book provides more specific information on medical expense insurance, the most common kind of health insurance in America. The text begins by describing the two coverages that provide health insurance to most Americans: group major medical insurance and individual hospital-surgical insurance. Subsequent chapters discuss the following topics: marketing and sales, pricing, contract provisions, underwriting, policy administration, claim administration, and industry issues.

Managed Care:
Integrating the Delivery and Financing of Health Care, Part A

An introduction to the field of managed health care, this book explains what managed care is, introduces the concepts on which it is based, and describes how it works in the real world. The book presupposes no prior knowledge of either managed care or insurance. Topics include the development of managed care, cost control techniques, measuring and improving quality, types of managed care organizations, and the involvement of government in managed care.

Managed Care:
Integrating the Delivery and Financing of Health Care, Part B

Part B of HIAA's managed care series covers operational issues and problems. Topics include the governance and management structure of managed care organizations; selective medical provider contracting; network administration and provider relations; marketing and member services; claims administration; financing, budgeting, and rating; legal issues; accreditation; and regulation.

Managed Care:
Integrating the Delivery and Financing of Health Care, Part C

Part C of this series examines current issues in managed care, operations and problems in specialized areas of managed care, and the role of managed care in government health benefit programs. Topics include public and private purchasing groups; consumers and physicians; managed care for pharmacy, dental, behavioral health, and vision benefits; and managed care for federal employees and military personnel, in the Medicare program, and in state government programs.

Supplemental Health Insurance

This book is intended to provide those who have a basic knowledge of health insurance and supplemental health insurance with more specific information on the major supplemental products in the marketplace. In addition, the gaps in health coverage that led to the need for additional insurance are discussed for each product. Topics include Medicare supplements, hospital indemnity coverage, specified disease insurance, accident coverage, dental plans, specialty plans, and the supplemental insurance market.

Health Care Fraud:
An Introduction to Detection, Investigation, and Prevention

This book provides an orientation in how health care fraud is perpetrated and what is being done to combat it. It looks at how some of the most common fraudulent schemes operate, how these schemes are detected and investigated, and the laws that can be brought to bear against them. Fraud perpetrated by health care providers, consumers, and others is included, and fraud involving not just medical expense insurance but also managed care and disability income insurance is covered.

THESE BOOKS MAY BE ORDERED
BY CALLING 800-828-0111.

The HIAA Insurance Education Program

Gregory F. Dean, JD, CLU, ChFC
Executive Director

Joyce Meals
Assistant Director

Leanne Dorado
Manager of Education Operations

Kevin Gorham
Fiscal Manager

La'Creshea Makonnen
CE Credit Manager

Yolaunda Janrhett
Registration Coordinator

Matthew Grant
Internet Coordinator